G000068604

The Genie
and the Fisherman

And Other Tales from
the Travelling People

Duncan and Linda Williamson

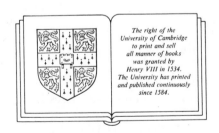

Cambridge University Press

Cambridge

New York   Port Chester   Melbourne   Sydney

to David

Published by the Press Syndicate of the University of Cambridge
The Pitt Building, Trumpington Street, Cambridge CB2 1RP
40 West 20th Street, New York, NY 10011, USA
10 Stamford Road, Oakleigh, Melbourne 3166, Australia

First published 1991

Printed in Great Britain at the University Press, Cambridge

Cover illustration by Jill Newton

British Library cataloguing-in-publication data
The Genie and the Fisherman and other tales from the travelling
people.
I. Williamson, Duncan 1928–   II.Williamson, Linda
823.914 [F]

ISBN 0 521 36212 1
ISBN 0 521 36981 9 pbk

AEB

Contents

Preface   4

Introduction   6
Words and Phrases from Traveller Speech   9
The Genie and the Fisherman   11
The Fox and the Goat   14
The Laird and the Crane   18
The Cockerel and the Fox   21
Jack goes back to School   24
The Dog and the Fox   28
Johnny McGill and the Frog   31
The Twelve Seasons   35
Thomas the Thatcher   40
Lion and the Four Bulls   43
The Princess and the Fox   48
The Boy and the Snake   55
House of the Seven Boulders   59
Seal Mother   64
Hooch for Skye!   73

Preface

Duncan Williamson's traveller tales, the stories he has collected aurally from the Travelling People of Scotland, are in extraordinary demand. Teachers in primary schools throughout Scotland and England invite him to tell traditional stories to no less than twelve thousand children every year! *The Genie and the Fisherman* is a collection of Duncan Williamson's favourites for schoolchildren, and it is presented in the manner of a visit to them. Duncan begins by narrating simple tales about tricksters and their greatest weapon in the face of adversity – wit. Animal stories are told for the very young which carry the noble spiritual truth – to think first on the needs of God's smallest creatures. Didactic stories are spun with magical charm so that their lessons spelling out the differences between love and greed are firmly implanted on the developing mind. 'Stronger' tales make up the last third of the collection – with moments of terror, fright and tragedy in the narratives – aimed at older children. The book ends with a mysterious Highland tale told in the vibrant language of the travelling storyteller; Jack, the travellers' hero, makes a mistake in 'Hooch for Skye!' that nearly costs him his life. But he succeeds in the end by virtue of his hard work and intelligence, aptitudes celebrated down through millennia in the culture of the travelling people.

The language of these stories when they are told is a dialect of Scottish English. I have anglicized them further so that schoolchildren of the ages eight to eleven can read them without difficulty. But the stories would lose much of their irresistible appeal as the tales of a traveller if every Scots and traveller usage were modified, or made to conform to a correct English standard. Thus I have retained an elementary level of non-English vocabulary in the text – and the child reader can become familiar with these words from the very start by scanning the list of words and phrases from traveller speech shown on pages 9–10.

I should like to acknowledge the support of the School of Scottish Studies (SSS), Edinburgh University, in the preparation of this book: 'The Cockerel and the Fox', 'The Twelve Seasons', 'Lion and the Four Bulls', 'Hooch for Skye!', 'Thomas the Thatcher', 'Seal Mother', 'The Boy and the Snake' and 'Jack goes back to School' were originally recorded on reel-to-reel tapes in 1976, 1978, 1985 and 1986; they are now lodged in the SSS sound archives. 'The Genie and the Fisherman', 'The Fox and the Goat', 'The Laird and the Crane' and 'The Dog and the Fox' were first published by Central Regional Council's Traveller Project in 1984 under the direction of Mrs Aimee Chalmers. They were among a set of twelve single story books illustrated throughout by the traveller children of Central Region who were attending a mobile education unit; the set is now out of print. 'Johnny McGill and the Frog', 'The Princess and the Fox' and 'House of the Seven Boulders' were recorded early in 1988 specifically for this collection.

All the stories in *The Genie and the Fisherman* have been transcribed directly from the recorded narrations of Duncan Williamson and virtually every word in the text is the narrator's. My thanks go to Ruth Cruikshank of Tayport and to Fred Kent of the School of Scottish Studies, who assisted me in the work of tape copying and transcribing.

Linda Williamson
Lizziewells, Collessie, Fife

Introduction

The Travelling People, a brief history

Six thousand years ago Britain was inhabited by 'hunter-gatherers', bands of people who lived a nomadic life travelling across the country hunting deer and seals in the winter-time, gathering nuts and berries in the summer-time. These people did not build any houses or try to settle anywhere. But certain places on the land were very important to them for religious reasons – these they claimed for themselves by putting stones down. The West Coast of Scotland was a favourite part of the country for hunters because its hills, caves and many wooded lochsides provided shelter, and because the sea was a source of food during winter months when trees and bushes were bare of fruit. By cooking shellfish, especially mussels, the oldest people of Scotland survived.

Farming was a way of life which never appealed to these early nomads. And when Scotland was settled about 4000 BC by newcomers from Northern Europe, who were mainly interested in grazing animals and growing crops, the travelling people kept apart from them by living on in their tents made of animal skins, finding and following different sources of food around the country which swelled or depleted with the change of seasons. But farmers continued to come in and settle Scotland, from Germany and Holland, and by 2000 BC they outnumbered the travelling people. The 'travellers' began to see that the settled community were growing vegetables and grain, having a better source of food than they had. Because the travellers wanted to have some of this food, they said, 'We must make something the settlers want and need.' So they started working in metals. They made metal spears for fishing and fishing hooks, arrowheads, knives and hatchets; they made crocks of iron for holding pots on the fire and they made pots. These were traded for grain and foodstuffs.

Iron was a metal easily melted and shaped, and the travelling people became experts at gathering the rocks of iron ore, melting down the iron, battering it out and making articles. In the Highlands the travellers became known as *ceaird*, metal workers. By the second century BC they had learned to wash the iron articles in tin – which made pots and pans and jugs look beautiful as if they were washed in silver. And the tinware kept clean because it could not rust like iron. But the travelling people also became fine craftsmen in other

6

mediums. They worked in horn and leather and willow – materials found at hand living close to nature. Spoons were made from horn, belts and laces from the deer hide; baskets were made from willow, necklaces from shellfish; brooches and bangles were made from the mother-of-pearl shell they fished from the freshwater rivers. These were all traded for food and goods, such as clothes and blankets, with house dwellers.

Over the past two thousand years the travelling people have managed to keep fast many of their age-old customs, special codes and general outlook on life. Death is a most sacred event, when passage to the Other World is carefully prepared. As a traveller you are buried with a little cup, a piece of bread and a coin. Death is a beginning of time, when you really come to *live*. You need your jug and your wee piece of bread with you to carry you on your journey and your silver coin to pay your way into the Land of Eternity. Birth is also a very important event among the travelling people. When news that a baby is born to a young couple reaches travellers, they will go and see – even if it means walking for miles – and bring what they can afford to the new baby. They do this because they believe *that* new baby might marry into their family, might become one of theirs, which naturally does happen among these people. All travellers are connected to each other in Scotland, connected to one extended kin group. Marriage is a very serious and strictly defined event. A man and woman are married according to traveller law once they spend a night together out of sight of their parents. And travellers marry for life. A young man who has a young wife can come in to an encampment of travellers, crack and tell stories, sit and make baskets and feel free. As a married traveller man or woman you enjoy all the privileges of being in and joining the family circle.

Children and the tradition of storytelling

The travelling children learned the crafts of their people, basketry and metal work, from the very earliest age, when they were able to sit next to their fathers and mothers. And as a child you grew up to revere Mother Nature, because Mother Nature was your primary teacher – She taught you how to collect berries, how to collect food, She grew animals and plants which supplied the materials for your making things. And Mother Nature gave you the cures from the herbs. The travelling people were known for their cures and their healing powers, and it was because they preferred to stick to their own beliefs and ways of thinking that the settled community came to distrust them. They were different.

For example, schools were not valued by the travelling community. Instead, stories were told and retold and passed on, stories were the education which gave you the lessons you needed to grow up to be a good person. Everyone needs to know things! And for solving any problem in life, a story tells you how; in every story there is a solution. And by this oral tradition the travelling life has come down to us today – from a beginning in time at least six thousand years ago. The first stories were there long before schools in Scotland were ever thought of, in the fourteenth and fifteenth centuries by the parish priests. A hunter would come and tell about his day; maybe he fell out of a tree or was chased by a boar and . . . that was a story! Everybody was interested in the experience and everyone's experience was a story. The people in the earliest times discussed their life with each other – this was the origin of stories. And today mothers tell stories to their lassies – about the beautiful princess, how she reacted, how she pleased her father or never pleased him, how she wanted this man and didn't want that one, how she fell in love. Mothers tell stories about castles and queens and maids and farmers' wives and cooks to their girls to teach them to grow up and be respectable. And fathers tell stories about Jack. Jack was sometimes lazy, sometimes he was clever, sometimes afraid, sometimes brave. But Jack always came out on top! And a son listening to his father and remembering his father's story will say today, 'If Jack could do it, so can I!'

And this was the idea of storytelling: an old man who knew a story would pass it on to his son. Because *he* had told it to his son with good heart and had felt good and happy when telling him a story, he wanted his son to tell *his* son the story in the same way! When I tell my father's stories I've got a great feeling coming through for me – that my father had told me that story because he was feeling good and he was happy, giving me something fine that I could pass on to my family or to anyone else who would care to listen. So when I do it in the same spirit of happiness, there is goodness being passed on. Storytelling makes people better. And in this spirit I wish to give you the following, the most treasured tales of my childhood from my travelling forebears.

Words and Phrases from Traveller Speech

The Travelling People of Scotland have their own way of speaking. They use many Scottish forms of English words, such as *o'* (of), *tellt* (told) and *wolfs* (wolves). In their speech the word 'of ' is often left out when they refer to quantity or amount: *plenty* (plenty of) and *wee drop* (small amount of). *An* is often used instead of *and*; and *in* may end words where *ing* would be used in English. Sometimes the storyteller's choice of words is influenced by the Gaelic language; for example, 'was just after bringing' (had just brought) is found in the Western Highlands, where Duncan Williamson grew up. Readers will clearly understand most words and phrases in the context of the stories, but those terms more foreign to English are explained below:

ainsel	self
alow	below
aside	beside
awa	away
awfae	awful
awfae, an	a lot of
ay	always
aye	yes; indeed
bit	bit of a (the)
but	and
by	in comparison with
catcht	took
cried	called
dinna(e)	do not
disna	doesn't
doubt	expect
etten	eaten
feart	afraid
flyer	cleverer
forbyes	as well; besides
gang	go
gets on to	attacks with words
hae	have
haet, a	nothing at all
happed	covered
I doubt	I expect
keeked; keeking	peeped; peeping
ken; kent	know; knew
landed	arrived
mind	remember
more the night	for the rest of the night
nane	none
no	not
nor	or
nothing	anything
past the common	better than average
prigged and preached	pleaded with and implored
puckle	small amount of
raiked	searched thoroughly through
speak to	trouble

9

that	who	*wee toy*	very small
this	these	*wi'*	with
to	at	*wir; wirselves*	our; ourselves
two-three	few	*yin*	one
was	were		

These are some traveller names for people, places and things:

burn	stream
camp	tent, camping gear
chap	stroke of the clock
cloots	blankets
clypes	lies, gossip
crack	talk, discuss; short story
dulse	edible seaweed
friends	relations, kinsfolk
gloamin	twilight
goose-girl	girl who walked across the land with geese long ago, selling and trading them on the way to market
grìosach	burning embers
henwife	old woman who stayed on her own and kept hens and ducks; said to have special powers
hooch	shout of excitement
laird	landlord
lochsides	shores of the sea lochs, or arms of the sea extending long distances inland
message; messages	errand; groceries
piece	sandwich
toorie	thing rising to a peak
wag-at-the-wall clock	pendulum clock
wean	wee one, child
welt	hit, blow to the head
wife	older woman
ye; yese	you (familiar) unstressed; you (fam. pl.)
youse	you (pl.)

The Genie
and the Fisherman

I heard this story from an old traveller when I was about fourteen,
when we used to gather together and tell old stories. The travellers
in those days had hundreds and hundreds and hundreds of stories –
and this very old tale is supposed to have been true.

There was once an old fisherman and his wife and they lived by the
side of the shore. He was very poor and used to go out every morning
– it was a hand-net he used for casting from the shore. In those old-
fashioned days the fishermen threw nets out into the sea to try and
catch some fish. But things began to get very hard for them and the
more he fished the less he got.

Every time he came back his wife would shout and argue with
him, 'You are a poor fisherman, ye cannae catch nothing! What are
we going to live on, how are we going to survive? You must try yer
best, rise up early in the morning and go out and catch some decent
fish! So we can sell some and have some to ourselves.'

And the poor old man did his level best. Every day he rose at
day-break and fished till dark. Some days he got nothing. And
whenever he came home without any fish his wife would shout and
argue and scold at him, tell him how useless as a fisherman he was –
how they were going to survive she didn't know. She told him he
would just have to keep on trying. So one morning he swore to
himself, 'I am going down to fish this morning and I am not going to
come back until I make it worthwhile!'

He cast his net in the sea and he fished, and he fished all day
and still got nothing. He was just getting fed up when he thought, 'I
will have one more go. I'll go along the beach a bit where I have
never fished before and try.'

11

And he cast his net once again, waited till it sunk into the water. He pulled his net in . . . but nothing, not one single fish in the net. But right in the corner of the net was an old-fashioned bottle, the oldest-fashioned clay bottle he had ever seen in his life. It was covered in seaweed it was so old. And the old man pulled his net, pulled it up on the beach and lifted out the bottle.

He looked round the bottle, he looked round the bottle and said to himself, 'I've never seen a bottle like this before in my life . . . it must be very old . . . I wonder if there is anything in it?' He never knew what it was meant for – there was an old glass, a kind of stone cork in it. And he took his old knife out of his pocket, picked the cork off. He put his nose to smell it to see what kind of stuff was in it, when out of the bottle came the smoke – dark dark smoke! And the old man was afraid. The smoke got bigger and bigger and rose in a cloud above his head. It began to take form . . . it turned into a genie, a real genie! And the old man was awful feart, oh, he was terrified.

The genie spoke to him in a stern voice, 'Old man, do you know what you have done?'

'No, no,' the old man said, 'no, I don't know what I have done – I never did any harm! I just caught this bottle in my net and I pulled it in, and I wanted to see what was inside the bottle. I took off the cork and now you have come out of it! What are ye?'

And the genie said, 'I am a genie! I am the Genie of This Bottle, and for seven hundred years I have been a prisoner in here! I was put in this bottle by my master, who was jealous of me hundreds of years before, and cast out into the sea. There I lay until you picked me up in yer net. For the first three hundred years I promised that the person who would take the bottle and let me out, I would make him the richest man in the world, I would give him gold and diamonds and silver for evermore. And still no-one took me out. For the second three hundred years I promised that I would make the man the king upon this land, I would give him everything that his heart desired if he would only rescue me from the sea. But still no-one picked me out of the sea. Then the last hundred years I swore that whoever took me out of the sea, I would kill him and make him so small – I would put *him* back in the bottle and throw *him* in the sea to suffer what I suffered. So *you* are the one! You are the one to set me free. So I am sorry, old man, but I have to kill you and put yer remains back in the bottle.'

'Well,' the old man said, 'I suppose if you are going to kill me

and put me back in the bottle, there is not much I can do about it –
seeing you are a big powerful genie, more powerful than me. But
before ye do that to me, will ye do one thing for me?'

'Yes,' said the genie, 'I'll do anything for ye. But don't ask me
to go back in the bottle!'

'No,' the old man said, 'I'm not asking ye to go back in the
bottle, I'm only wondering . . .'

'And what are ye wondering?' said the genie.

'That a person as big as you could come out of that small
bottle . . . I can't believe it no way, that a person as large as you
could come out of that bottle so small. So just to see that ye are
telling me the truth, would ye do me one favour before ye kill me?'

'Well,' said the genie, 'I will grant ye that.'

'Would ye just show me how ye managed to get in that bottle?'

And the genie said, 'Well, just to ease yer mind – before I put
ye in the bottle and put ye back in the sea for the rest of the days of
yer life, I'll show ye . . .' And the genie went into a long strip of
smoke, he went back into the bottle slowly, slowly, slowly, till every
part of him disappeared in the bottle.

Then the old man ran and he put the cork back into the bottle,
screwed it tight with his knife. He catcht it and threw it as far as he
could out into the sea! And there the bottle lies for the rest of time.
(But if ye are walking by the shore and ye see a bottle lying, just be
very careful when ye lift it. Because ye never know – it might be the
genie in that bottle!)

So, not to be beaten, the old man said, 'Well, that was bad
luck for me, but I'll have another shot again,' and he cast his net once
more. Lo and behold, he could hardly pull it in it was so loaded with
fish! He counted the fish – there were twenty-one fish in his net. And
he carried them all back to his wife. His wife was so happy that she
cooked some for him and some for herself and made the old man go
to the village, sell the rest of them next morning for some money.
And the funny thing was – from that day on the old man and his wife
never had another bad day. Every day the old man went to fish and
cast his net off the shore, sure enough there never was a day he threw
his net in the sea that he never caught some fish! And he said to
himself, 'Maybe,' he said, 'the genie did bring me luck!'

And what do you think then, did the genie bring him luck or
did the genie bring him bad luck? Because I think the genie brought
him good luck! And that's the last of my wee story.

The Fox
and the Goat

An old uncle of mine, Sandy Reid, told me this old tale when I was only about five years old on the shores of Loch Fyne. He was a great storyteller who travelled every summer to Argyll.

It was a fine summer's morning and the old fox wakened in his den. He stretched himself. He'd had a great supper the night before in the rocks, and where he had his den was warm and hot. He felt thirsty, so he said, 'I must get up and go and have a drink in the first little brook that I come to because I am very thirsty this morning.'

He came out and stretched himself again. It was the middle of June and already the rocks were hot with the sun. So he went to look for a drink in the first stream that he came to, but all the streams were dry. The sun had dried them all up, and the fox wandered for nearly half a day but couldnae find a drink. He got more thirsty; the further he went the thirstier he got. So he said, 'I must find a drink some place!' But no. He searched as far as he could – all the water was dried up – no drink. So he sat down and his tongue was hanging out dry.

He thought and he thought, where was the nearest pool or lake or stream that he could get to without being seen? He said, 'There is only one place . . . that is down at the farm. And down at the farm there lives my enemy, the farmer. If he sees me he will shoot me because farmers do not like foxes running about their farms. They are afraid of us killing their hens.' But finally the thirst got the better of him and he made his way down to the farm.

Now in those bygone days the farmers didnae have any water inside the houses. They had these wells outside the farm. And on the wells they had what you call a 'windlass' with a rope and two buckets:

14

this rope lowered one bucket down and you pulled it up; then you reversed it and lowered the other bucket down, and pulled it up. As one bucket went down the other one came up.

The fox crawled his way down to the farm hiding himself as much as possible. Finally he made his way to the well thinking that the farmer would have left a wee drop water in the bucket. When he landed there the two buckets were dry. One was down in the well and the other bucket was up at the top. He looked down into the well, he saw the beautiful clear crystal water. He longed for one taste of that water.

He was not hungry, he was thirsty. And he thought and he thought, 'How can I get a drink? Because I can't do what the farmer does, wind the handle and call up the bucket, wind it up. Probably if I jumped in the bucket it would take me down into the well, then I could drink until my heart's content.'

At last he decided the only way he was going to get a drink was to jump in the bucket. So he jumped in, and the weight of him took the bucket right into the well, which was about ten feet down from the ground. The bucket landed right side up in the well. And the fox leaned over and he licked, he licked and he licked – all this beautiful clear water – until he was finally contented. He lay in the bucket fully contented . . . then it dawned on him. He looked up, he could see the sun shining above him in the well.

'Now,' he says, 'I am a silly old fox. I was so dry and thirsty that I never gave it a thought: I foolishly jumped in the bucket, and now I am down in the well how am I going to get up? How am I going to get out of this bucket? There is no way I'm going to climb up there! And the first person that is going to come along will be the farmer, he is going to wind up the bucket for water. And sure enough if he gets me in his bucket he is going to shoot me! Because farmers do not like foxes very much, we are farmers' enemies.' Now he begins to get worried. He sits and he sits, he sits in the bucket; the day passes by. He knows from past experience that the farmer always comes late in the evening for two buckets of water.

But unknown to him an old goat belonging to the farmer was having the same trouble: he was thirsty with the sunshine and he too wanted a drink. He knew that the farmer always drew water from the well, and after having searched all round the farm he thought, 'There is only one place I'll get a drink – that is at the well. Because the farmer always leaves a little water in his bucket.' So the old goat made his way to the well. (This was an old goat the farmer had had for years, a pet for his children. And it just wandered around the farm

15

doing what it pleased.)

When he landed at the well, one bucket was up and the other was down. He looked in the bucket and there was nothing – it was dry. Then he looked into the well: what he saw was old Mister Fox sitting in the bucket.

Now the fox was sitting looking up and the goat was at the top looking down. Now the fox and the goat were good friends, because all animals really are; they never really hurt each other unless they want something to eat. That is the only time they kill, when they need something to eat.

So the old goat looked down and said, 'Hello, Mister Fox!' in the best voice he could put on.

And the fox looked up surprised, because he thought it was the farmer at first. He said, 'Hello, Mister Goat!' Then he thought, 'I will have to work something here, I'll have to work up a fast plan.'

The goat said, 'What are you doing down there, Mister Fox?'

And the fox said, 'Oh, Mister Goat, you have no idea how lovely it is down here in this beautiful well beside this lovely clear water!'

The old goat's tongue is hanging out for a drink – he's really thirsty.

'You have no idea how the shade is so cool,' said the fox; 'there is no sunshine. The well is so lovely and the water so cool – I just want to stay here for ever and ever and ever!'

The goat said, 'I'm so thirsty, Mister Fox. I wonder how could I get a drink?'

And the fox said, 'I cannae give you a drink because I am enjoying myself too much. I cannae give you a drink!'

'Well,' the goat said, 'Mister Fox, please try to help me – I'm thirsty! I can hardly stand it any more.'

'Well,' the fox said, 'seeing you are a great friend of mine and you and I have never been enemies, why don't you join me? Then both of us can sit in the well and we can talk, have a nice good crack and have a good drink!'

'How can we do that?' said the goat.

'Well,' said the fox, 'there is no problem. All you need to do is jump in the bucket and come down beside me!'

So the goat said, 'Do you think I could manage it?'

'Och, that is no trouble! If I can do it you can do it – you are bigger than me and heavier than me, Mister Goat. And if I can jump in the bucket . . .' (because they were large wooden buckets, ye know, and they held about four or five gallons of water).

16

So the goat climbs into the bucket. It is just poised above the well, and with the weight of the goat – down goes the bucket into the well. When the goat's bucket goes into the well, up goes the fox's because the fox is lighter than the goat. And the goat's bucket splashes in the top of the water. The goat is no worrying – he is leaning over and licking up, drinking up this beautiful water.

Now, when the fox's bucket goes up the fox is so glad he jumps out when it reaches the top. He stands for a wee while; he looks down at the goat. The goat is busy drinking away. Until the goat has drunk enough the fox waits, because he knows fine he is free and has plenty time to spend. He is not even hungry. He looks down . . . and he never felt sorry for the goat because he knew the farmer would not touch the goat when he got him in the well in the bucket. So he said, 'Are you enjoying yourself, Mister Goat?'

'Oh,' he said, 'Mister Fox, I am enjoying myself! The water is so cool. But why did you not wait beside me? You promised you would wait beside me and we could talk about things, have a nice long talk!'

'Well,' said the fox, 'I am really sorry. But you see, your weight was the cause of the trouble, because when you went in the bucket you were so heavy that you pulled me up. And I have no way of getting down to ye: even if I jumped back in the bucket I still couldnae come down beside ye.'

And the goat said, 'That is all right for you – you are up out of the well now. I've had my drink, now I would like to get up and get something to eat.'

'Well,' the fox said, 'Mister Goat, I will have to get on my way. I can't tarry any longer, because you know what happens to me if the farmer comes and finds me here – he will shoot me!'

And then the goat said, 'What about me, Mister Fox? I am your friend. You are not going off to leave me here all by myself in this well?'

The fox said, 'There is not much I can do about it.'

'Please, please tell me – what can I do?' pleaded the goat.

So the fox looked down. He said, 'Well, Mister Goat, there is only one thing I can tell you . . .'

'Tell me, please!' said the goat. 'Tell me please!'

The fox said, 'Just sit in the bucket and wait till *a silly old goat* comes along and jumps in the other bucket! Then you will probably get up here where I am right now!' At that the fox strutted off home to his den in the rocks. And that is the last of my story.

17

The Laird
and the Crane

I heard this one a long time ago when I was young, only about five or six. Aye, it is one my father told me, one of his favourites. I always remembered my father's stories, they just stuck with me all the time.

Many many years ago there once lived this laird. He had a large estate and loved hunting. He used to invite all these guests to come and hunt with him and they hunted all over his estate. So one day he called his friends together and said, 'Come, we will have a great ball and a great hunt! Bring all my friends and friends of friends, we will have a great time!'

But before the day they arrived he was out by himself one morning, and he saw a crane, a large crane by the riverside fishing in the water. And the laird said, 'That would be a nice feast for us when my friends come to visit me – we could have that crane for lunch.' So he took his gun and he shot the crane. He took it home, carried it into the cook and told him, 'I'm having a great party, I have friends coming from all over and I would like you to take this crane and cook it as best as you can. Make sure you bring it in and put it at my table when all my friends arrive!'

'Certainly!' said the cook, 'I'll do that for you, my lord.'

So the day of the great feast arrived; the great guests began to arrive at the laird's castle. They sat and they talked and they drank and they wined and they talked about their hunts, their fights and everything until it came along about evening. It was time for dinner.

But as I tell ye, the cook had made such a beautiful job of cooking the crane, it looked so nice and so delicious he just couldnae help himself – he said, 'I would love to have a little bit of that crane!

18

It looks so delicious, it looks so nice. Why should just the laird have this? And me, his faithful cook who has been with him for years and years can't enjoy just a little morsel of this crane!' But temptation got the better of him and he took a leg of the crane – he ate it and he enjoyed it. He put the rest of the crane back in the tureen.

The laird called for dinner for himself and dinner for all his guests. Naturally, the cook brought in the crane, carried the silver tureen right to the table, placed it down before the laird. The laird lifted the lid off the tureen and looked: he saw the crane lying there with one leg. He was so upset he put the lid back on the top and told his cook, 'Cook,' he said, 'you have disgraced me before my friends! Take that away and I will deal with you later!'

So the poor cook felt terrible. He took the tureen with the crane back into the kitchen and then fetched in something else. The party went on until late in the evening, and when all the guests departed to their own homes the cook was immediately sent for. When he landed in front of his master, his master was so angry the cook felt afraid. 'What is it, master?' he said. 'What is the trouble?'

'The trouble,' said the master, 'is – *you* are in trouble! How dare you before my friends and guests send me in a crane that I specially shot for my own evening meal with one leg! How dare you take a leg from my crane!'

'But, master,' said the cook, who was a man a little bit witty and found the only excuse possible to save his face, 'but, master, a crane does only have one leg!'

And the laird stood, said, 'What did you say?'

He said, 'Master, a crane only has one leg: every crane I see when I go out walking or go with you for a hunt, when it stands in the river it only has one leg. How can I make two legs on a crane when it only has one?'

'That is not true!' said the laird.

'Well, master,' he said, 'as far as I know it is true, for all the cranes that I have ever seen have only one leg.'

So they argued for a while, but the laird couldnae convince the cook that a crane had two legs. And the cook knew in his own heart he was guilty, but he was trying to get out of it as best as he could. So the laird being a fair man he said to his cook, 'All right, tomorrow morning at the break of dawn I am taking you on a hunt. I'll show you that a crane has two legs and then you'll know you are guilty.'

'Fair enough, master,' said the cook. 'I'll be ready when you are.'

So, true to his word, the laird rose at the break of dawn and called the cook. They had a little breakfast and both of them got the horses and guns. They went out on a hunt in the morning, and they had not gone far until they came to a small stream. Sure enough – standing there was a crane fishing in the burn. (And ye know, when cranes fish and have to wait for a while, they usually stand on one leg – they get a better balance that way.) There was a crane standing on one leg.

'Look, master,' said the cook, 'there is your crane and it only has one leg!'

'That's not true,' said the laird, 'that crane has two legs! Just you wait and see, I'll prove it to you.' And the master jumped off his horse, walked to the burnside and clapped his hands, shooed the crane away. Naturally, when he shooed the crane away the crane put down his other leg and flew off. He turned round to the cook and said, 'Now do you see that the crane has two legs?'

'Well, master,' he said, 'I have only one thing to say . . .'

'Before I punish you,' said the laird, 'you'd better say it!'

'Master,' he said, 'if you had clapped your hands at the dinner table, probably the crane would have put down his other leg; then this would never have happened.'

The laird had nothing to say, he knew he was beat. And he turned round to his cook and said, 'My man, your wit has saved you!' And from that day on till the end of time the laird and the cook became the greatest of friends. And that is the end of my wee story.

The Cockerel
and the Fox

*I remember my daddy telling me this wee story. Och, the cracks
and tales they used to tell round the campfires long ago, there were
hundreds and thousands of them. Parents would take turns, you
see, telling stories, and we children used to sit and listen curled up
to the fire.*

On this farm there was a big cockerel. And this cockerel had a wife
an about half a dozen o' wee chickens. They were picking round
about the farm all day. But in these days farmers didna keep nae
hen-houses or nothing. And the cockerel was ay telling the hen,
'Look,' (he could speak to her an that) 'you'd better keep an eye to
these wee weans!' (The father cried them 'weans', or children – they
were weans to them.) 'Keep an eye to them because you ken the foxes
an things comin down from the hill would snap you awa in a minute.
An eagles! I cannae be guarding you all the time, ye ken,' he said to
the hen. 'I've got to scrape an look for my bit livin the same as you.'
    She said, 'I'm doing my best. How about you watching them
for a wee while?'
    'Aye,' he said, 'I'm doing my best too. Well, I'll tell ye,
they're beginning to grow now and we'd better draw them all round
about us an tell them this wee story.'
    So the cockerel sat down on this wee branch and the hen sat
aside him. And he gathered all the wee chickens round about him. He
said, 'Look, weans, come here! I want to tell you a wee story. When I
was wee wi' my father years and years ago I stayed on this farm too.
And like me, my father was here wi' my mother too. There were
eight o' us. And me being a wee bit bigger than the rest, I was a wee
bit flyer than the rest o' them.' Now all the wee chickens were sitting

listening on top of the branch, and the hen was sitting. 'My father tellt me to watch for foxes,' said the cockerel. 'But we didna ken what foxes was in them days when I was young.' And all the wee chickens were curled up aside their mother, ye ken? And they were listening to their father telling the story.

The cockerel said, 'So my father didna care very much, he didna watch us very much. We were runnin about the stockyard pickin here an pickin there, an he never looked after us at night-time or a haet. My poor old mother, she looked after us better than him. But anyway, down come a fox yin night – snapped ane o' my brothers awa. Now there were only seven o' us left. My mother went into an awful state, but my father didna bother so much. Man, my father was a fool! But on the farm where we stayed was a big spruce tree, and every night we used to climb up on a branch an sit on a branch so that nae beast could get us, me an my brothers and sisters.

'But yin night we were just going to hop on a branch when down came the fox and nicked awa another brother belongin to me! Now there were only six o' us left. And I was the only laddie. But I was a wee bit older than the rest. But my father was a fool! We all hopped up on the branch at night. My mother gathered us all together and took us up on this branch, here we were sittin. We looked down just on this moonlit night – here's a fox comin. And he came right in below the tree where we were all sittin. He stopped. He cracked to my father.

'He said to my father, "What are ye doin sittin up there? Come on down, man, and hae a wee bit crack! I'll tell ye where I was, and you can tell me what you've been doin all day."

'But my father being kind o' soft-wittit, he hopped down on another lower branch, an he's cracking away to the fox. An him an the fox got to be good pals.

'Fox said, "Man, I keep stretchin my neck to tell ye a wee story. Can ye no come down a wee bit closer so's I'll no need to reach up to crack to ye?"

'My father hopped down to another branch. So him an the fox cracked away again for another long while. But the fox sat that way, an he coaxed an he coaxed an he coaxed till he got my father down, right down to the last low branch. And he says to my father, "Listen, I'll tell ye another wee story."

'My father got interested an he hopped down aside him. That's the last time I ever saw my father! The fox went away wi' hi. Now my mother was left wi' the wee weans and she had to rear us all up her ainsel. My sisters were sellt. But I was the only brother and I was kept. Now,' says the cockerel, 'I'll no be so silly as what my father was! Come on, it's gettin kind o' gloamin. Come on, we'll go to the tree.'

He hops up the tree. He's sitting in the tree . . . first thing comes down is a fox! He says to the hen, 'Look, look comin down there – a fox! Get the weans hopped onto the next branch. I'm no as soft as my father was,' this big cockerel said.

In comes the fox, stops below the tree. 'Aye,' he says, 'it's a fine night.'

'Aye,' says the cockerel, 'it's a fine night.'

Fox said, 'Eh, what's about comin down for a wee crack?'

'Na, no me,' Cockerel said, 'I'm no comin down for nae crack. It's too cold down there more the night. The moon's too bright, you never ken who's knockin about . . . dangerous folk.'

'Dangerous folk!' he said. 'There's naebody here to speak to ye, man. It's only me, a wee fox who wouldna speak to ye – I wouldna touch ye!'

'Aye,' he said, 'ye never ken who would touch ye – you could be as bad as the rest.'

'Na, na,' Fox said, 'I wouldna touch ye. Come on down! I'll tell ye a wee story, where I've been and where I've no been, and who I've seen, how many folk I've seen.'

Cockerel said, 'Did ye see yin body passin here a minute ago?'

'No,' he said, 'I never seen nae – who was it?'

He says, 'A man wi' a gun an two dogs passed there just now, passed by this tree a wee minute ago. I dinna ken what he was lookin for.'

'Ah,' Fox said, 'he might be lookin for me! It's a good job you didna come down. If I'd hae got ye down here, you would hae never hae got back!' And that's the last o' the wee story.

Jack goes
back to School

I first heard this story from my father, but it was a favourite of all the old storytellers. Today, children like my ten-year-old daughter Betsy have found it fun and easy to learn, to tell to their friends.

After many many years Jack had grown very old. He had a family. His wife had died, and he came to live with his youngest daughter in a little cottage by the roadside. She had five or six little children. And these children loved their grandfather old Jack very very much. They sat in his lap and he told them stories, he told them about how he'd spent his entire life, how he'd met his wife and how he had travelled all over the world, how he'd met goblins and elves, and every night was a different story! These children were enthralled with Jack, wi' Grandad's stories, old Jack. He put them to sleep every night in bed. And his daughter Mary, she loved her father. Her husband said, 'Look, we dinna need to worry as long as he's with the children.' And sometimes the children fell asleep in his lap by listening to his stories.

But in these bygone days there were no cars on the road, it was all horses and carriages. But where he lived, Jack's son-in-law, Mary's husband, was a woodcutter, and he went out to cut wood every day. And old Jack he said to himself, while his son-in-law was at work and the children were in school, he would work in the garden. He would tidy up the garden an grow vegetables. He was more than eighty years old, and he was still Jack!

But one day he was working in the garden when lo and behold he saw a coach, four horses and a coach passing by. And he saw something falling from the coach. The horses drove on. He stepped out o' the garden and he walked out to the road. It was a rough old road in these bygone days. And lo and behold there was a handbag, a

24

permanty they called it in these days, a carrying bag. It's lying in the road! Jack picked it up, it was heavy. He opened it up. It was full, full of money. He carried it back, he took it in. His daughter was busy working in the kitchen. He went up to his bedroom and he hid it under his bed. Jack rubbed his hands together. He said, 'I've got golden sovereigns for evermore! Nobody's going to get them from me . . . I'm still Jack!'

Now he had a plot in his head. He said to himself, 'Look, I know where it's come from. This is the tax collection – people collecting the taxes around the town and the country. And it fell off the coach. But,' he said, 'it's mine.' Now Jack being Jack, he wanted to know how in the world he could come to keep this money. So being Jack he got an idea in his head. All day he sat in his room and he thought about it. And then the children came back from school that day.

The laddies and lassies, they all gathered round grandfather as usual and they said, 'Grandad, tell us a story, tell us a story!'

He said, 'I'll tell yese a story.' He tellt them stories past the common till they fell asleep.

But the next morning at breakfast time he said to his daughter, 'Mary, my lassie, I'm going back to school.'

She says, 'Dad, you canna go back to school!'

He says, 'I'm going back to school – this morning I go! Give me a pair o' scissors.'

She says, 'What are you wanting scissors for, Dad?'

He says, 'To clip my trousers short.'

She says, 'Dad, have you gone crazy?'

'No,' he said, 'I'm no going crazy. Give me a pair of scissors!' He got a pair o' scissors and he clipped his trousers above his knee. He said, 'Weans! Come here a minute, have you any old schoolbags lying about?'

'Aye, Grandad,' they said, 'we have. There's two-three schoolbags there.'

He says, 'Have you any books lying about you're no wanting?'

'Aye, Grandad,' they said.

Mary said, 'Where are you going?'

He said, 'I'm going with the weans to school.'

'Oh no, Grandad,' they said, 'you canna go!'

'I'm going with youse to school today,' he says. He cut the trousers short, put them on his legs, he got a bag from the weans, he got two books, he put the bag on his back and he went with the

25

weans. They walked to school, and he sat in the classroom with the weans in school.

The teacher said, 'What are you doing here, Jack?'

'Aye,' he said, 'I'm back to school. I want to learn to read, same as the weans, learn to read.' But anyway, he sat in the school all day with his short trousers on, with his schoolbag and his books. And he sat with the weans for one day in the school.

But he walked back with the weans that night and he told them stories. He did everything, put his bag away. And the next morning he was out in the garden as usual. The weans were off to school. He never went back to school anymore. Only one day he had gone to school.

But sure and behold he's in the garden close to the road when what should come driving up but another coach! Two men and their long hats and batons hanging down by their pockets. They pulled in. They stopped the coach by the side of the road. They came and said, 'Old man, you're busy.'

'Yes,' Jack said, 'I'm busy.'

'Well,' one said, 'you know who we are, we're the justices o' the peace, justices o' the peace.'

'Oh,' he said, 'I see, I can see by your coats and your tails and your batons you're justices of the peace.'

'The problem is, old man,' they said, 'the problem is we want to talk to you. The coach passed here two days ago. And we have lost a permanty with a lot of money, it fell off the coach. Have you by any chance seen it?'

'Oh,' Jack said, 'that's true. I saw it!'

'Oh you did?' they said. 'Oh,' the one looked to the other, 'ye've seen it?'

Jack said, 'Aye.'

He said, 'Have you any idea where it is?'

'Well,' he said, 'I saw it, eh, let me see now . . . The four horses and the coach passed by. It fell off and I picked it up, I carried it up an I put it alow my bed.'

'That's good enough,' said the two men, 'we have the right person. We've got him, right. Do you still have it?'

'Oh,' he said, 'I still have it.'

'But,' one says, 'when did this happen?'

'Well,' he says, 'wait a minute now, it was the day afore I went to school.'

He said, 'Old man, what do you mean?'

Jack said, '*The day afore I went to school!*'

He said, 'How old are you, old man?'

'Well,' he said, 'I'll be eighty-six on my birthday. Come my birthday I'll be eighty-six!'

And he said, 'When did you pick up the bag with the money?'

'Well,' he says, 'the day before I went to school I picked up the bag!'

And one justice says to the other, 'Look, come on, let's stop wasting wir time with a silly old fool!' And they drove on.

And Jack was left with the bag of money. He shared it with his wee daughter and they lived happy ever after!

The Dog
and the Fox

This is a very old tale and was told to me many years ago by my mother's brother Duncan. He was a great storyteller, old Duncan Townsley. He belonged to Argyll.

The old fox had lain in his den all day and he was hungry; because the days before he had been out hunting he had got very little to eat. In fact he was terrified, because he had been hunted twice by gamekeepers. Nightfall was approaching and he said to himself, 'Well, I will have to get something before night, because when it gets dark I'm not going to have much of a chance – all the birds will be roosting and all the rabbits will be in their burrows – I had better go out and get something to eat!'

So away went the old fox. He wandered here, he wandered there, he wandered everywhere that he thought he could find some game for himself to kill. But he could find nothing. He travelled on all his familiar paths, all his old hunting places. But not a hare, not a rabbit, nothing could he find. And the more he wandered the hungrier he got. Evening was approaching fast. So he sat down, considered for a while; he knew that he wasn't going to find anything to eat that night. He said to himself, 'There is only one thing I'll have to do.'

He knew it wasn't very far away to the nearest farm because he could see the lights in the distance. But he was kind of afraid to go near the farm in case the farmer was around with his gun – might shoot him for hunting some of his hens. 'If I could only see my old cousin the dog,' he said to himself. 'He probably has an old bone lying about, or maybe he has no finished his evening meal and would share it with me.' So he finally made up his mind to go as quietly as he could, go and visit his old friend Cousin Dog at the farm. He knew there was no other way he was going to get anything that night.

28

Away he went walking up the lane as stealthily as he could so that nobody could see him. Finally he came to the farm and round to the front where he knew his old cousin, old Dog, had his kennel. By good luck he never encountered the farmer. As he came round the corner to the front of the farm the first person he met was his old cousin Dog. And the farmer was just after bringing the old dog his supper. It was lying in a little dish beside the dog's kennel – there were bones and pieces of meat, all kinds, lying in the dog's dish. The fox saw this and it just made his mouth water!

So he said, 'Hello, Cousin Dog, how are you?'

And the dog said, 'Oh it's yersel, old Fox!'

'Aye,' he said, 'it is.'

'And what puts ye down here at this time o' night? I thought you would be away hiding out in yer old den up in the cliffs for the night,' said old Dog.

'Well, to tell ye the truth,' said the fox, 'the only reason I've come to visit ye – and ye know it is not often I come to see ye – I'm asking . . . I just came to ask ye a favour.'

'Well,' said the dog, 'we're friends, we're relations. And ye never trouble me very often. If there is anything ye want and I can help ye out, I'll try my best. What is yer favour?'

'Well,' the fox said, 'I have been hungry all day. In fact, I am so hungry I am no able to hunt. The gamekeeper hunted me all day yesterday, never gave me a chance to eat. I am so hungry I can barely walk. I just came down to see ye, to see if ye had an old bone lying abo⌐ and any bits of scraps of food ye could spare a poor hungry cousin.'

'Oh,' the dog says, 'if that's all that's troubling ye, there is plenty here! There's my supper, I've had plenty to eat and I'm no hungry. I'm just about to go for a sleep for the night, and if I dinnae eat it up the farmer will think "what's wrong wi' him?" And he'll no give me any more for breakfast. So help yerself!'

So the fox got into this dish of food, he just guzzled it up as fast as he could. He felt a bit better after he had licked the dish clean. So he and the dog sat and they talked for a wee while.

'Ye know,' the dog said to him, 'Cousin Fox, you are in the wrong kind of life.'

'An what makes ye think that?' the fox said.

'Well,' he said, 'look at me here: I sit here and I get plenty to eat, I have a nice warm kennel and plenty straw to sleep in, I get plenty of food, plenty to drink, plenty bones and I have got a great life! You'll have to change yer ways.'

The fox said, 'Ah certainly! What have ye got to do for all this? Ye must do something, ye cannae just stay on the farm all the days of yer life and do nothing for all this food and this good bed ye get, this nice kennel and everything ye do.'

'Well,' he said, 'I guard the farm. And if anybody, any strangers or anybody comes about at night, I bark and waken the farmer up, let him know if there is anybody around about the farm.'

'Ahem,' the fox says, 'well, that is no a very hard job.'

'No,' the dog said, 'the fact is I enjoy my life and I like it here.'

'Well,' said the fox, 'what would I need to do for to get the same kind of job that you've got?'

'Well,' the dog said, 'the first thing ye have got to do is come on down and see the farmer.'

'But if I come and see the farmer,' he said, 'he probably will shoot me, because I am a fox and farmers don't like foxes!'

'Well, that's true,' said the dog. 'But the main thing ye have got to get first is – ye have got to get a kennel.'

'Well,' the fox said, 'I like yer kennel, it is fine and warm and comfortable.'

'And then,' he says, 'ye get yer collar and yer chain.'

'What did you say?' said the fox.

He says, 'Ye get yer collar, a nice leather collar round yer neck and a chain.'

'And what's the collar and chain for?' says the fox.

'Well,' he says, 'to tie ye up.'

'Tie ye up?' says the fox.

'Yes,' he says, 'tie ye up!'

'And ye mean to say ye stay tied up there all day with a collar and chain round yer neck, tied up like a slave?'

'Aye,' said the dog, 'that's what I do – I'm tied up. Except sometimes when my master lets me out and takes me out for a walk for exercise. But never mind being tied up,' said the dog, 'life is quite good and yer belly is never empty!'

'Ah no,' said the fox, 'no me, old Cousin Dog! I like yer food and I like yer bed and I like yer home. But,' he said, 'I like my freedom best! So I will be bidding ye good-bye, old Dog. But thanks very much for the supper. If I ever have the chance to come and see ye again, I will return and see ye some other time. But ye will never get me tied up with a chain or a collar for all the food and all the beds in the world. For freedom is the thing that I love!'

At that the fox was gone, and the dog never saw him anymore. And that is the last of my story.

Johnny McGill
and the Frog

*Nobody knew where Johnny McGill came from. Some said he was
a veterinary student who was the son of a rich man in England.
His father and mother were ashamed of him because he had
married a gypsy woman. And Johnny loved this woman, he
brought her to Scotland. They used to pass through Argyll during
my grandfather's time, back before World War I, and the words
that were painted on his handcart said 'From Land's End to John
o' Groats twenty-two times on foot'. Johnny was a wandering vet
who just lived like a traveller. Mary, his wife, walked with wares
from door to door and sold things from her basket. She was a
fortune-teller. But he had no ambition in the world, Johnny didn't
want to own anything or have any riches. His one love in life was
looking after animals – all kinds, birds, the very mice, rats,
anything that walked on four legs – Johnny McGill took care of.
There were seagulls and crows with broken wings, even fish he
was known to cure. He set out in his life to take care of all the
little creatures who could not take care of themselves. Once on a
camping place Johnny never left till the sick animal he was
tending was as right as rain. I'm telling ye, he was known to have
carried a sick roe deer on his barrow for four days, hurled on the
top of his cloots and his camp, pulled on his wee handcart behind
him! But when he was finished with it, the deer was grazing and
picking the grass along the roadside. He said, 'Well, now I've
done my bit for you,' and he let it go. The deer went back to the
wild, but many years later it returned to him. Oh, there's some
great stories about Johnny McGill! The things Johnny did always
turned out good for him; all the little creatures he sorted had a way
of paying Johnny back, and Johnny said that it was in more
important things than money. The travellers believed he was a*

31

*great man, a wonderful man. They said he had 'hands of gold',
the way he treated bairns with whooping cough or measles. But he
was never really accepted, taken into the heart of travelling life,
because he was too clever for them. With all his bottles and
cordials travellers thought he might have been in league with the
'burkers' or body-snatchers, who came in the dark of night seeking
freshly killed human bodies for medical research. And it was not
until Johnny McGill up and disappeared, after years had passed
by, that all the good stories and good tales and good cracks came to
light. Johnny had gained great respect among the travelling people
once they came to know him, and he had many many friends – my
grandfather was one of his dearest. That's why I have so many
tales today of the legend of the travelling vet, Johnny McGill!*

One morning Johnny and his old wife were walking along as usual,
with a little handcart, travelling on to . . . no-one knows where,
wherever they could find a nice resting place by the roadside. Johnny
had picked up a few things on his travels, a bird with a broken wing
and little creatures he had mended on his way while his old wife sat
patiently. And he let them go. But the ones who were seriously
damaged he always carried with him.

So the place they came to this morning was an old farm track,
and Johnny was pushing his small handcart along when he stopped.
And his wife who was beside him, old Mary, wondered why he had
stopped so suddenly. For there before them Johnny saw a common
frog. And Johnny could see that the frog had been tramped on either
by some cattle beast or by a horse or a rider who had paid no
attention. But Johnny's eyes had seen that it was in trouble. So he
bent down quietly to pick up the frog.

Mary said, 'Johnny, what are ye doing?'

He said, 'Mary, my dear, it's a frog.'

She said, 'I know, Johnny. But it's just a frog.'

'Oh, Mary, it might be just a frog to you but,' he said, 'it's
another creature to me. Ye know, Mary, they all feel pain and they all
suffer. But no-one pays much attention to them, do they?' So he
picked up the frog and he could see that one of its hind legs was
broken. Johnny said, 'Mary, it won't cause any trouble, I'll just take
it along with us till we find the next camping place.' So he put the
frog on his little handcart in a safe place where it would not fall out,
and he travelled on.

32

He hadna gone far when he came to a little spot along the roadside which was derelict ground. 'Johnny,' said Mary, 'we'll stay here tonight.'

He said, 'I dinna see any fire marks. There's no been any travellers around.' Johnny was always interested in the travelling community, though they were not interested in him very much. They were kind of dubious about him because he was so clever and not one of their kind. So he pulled in his little handcart, put up his tent, kindled his fire and Mary made some supper. And Johnny McGill was a great reader.

So they sat and talked for a while. Then Johnny said, 'Mary, I've something to do.' And he got to his frog. He took it, examined the frog all up and down, across its leg. He said, 'Little fella, yer leg's broken. Ye're no good like that, ye'll never hop again unless we do something for ye. But don't worry, little friend, I'll soon fix ye.' So he set very carefully with some thread and some matchsticks, he bound and set the frog's leg. 'Now,' he said, 'little fella, ye'll be okay. My old wife and me has travelled far this last two weeks, an we'll just sit here and rest for a while, unless the police come along an move us on.' Which the police seldom ever did to Johnny McGill because he was well known in the West Coast.

Johnny stayed there for two weeks attending to his frog while old Mary called the houses, sold her clothes pegs, leather laces and anything she had from her little basket. She told fortunes and she was quite happy. Johnny attended to many little creatures forbyes his frog. But one evening they sat up late in their little tent, and all the light they had, because it was near winter-time, was a candle. Johnny was reading from a book, an because he was tired he had placed the frog by his feet in a little box. Then he got tired reading his book and he placed it by his side. He quietly dozed over to sleep.

But unknown to Johnny the candle burned down. And there was some straw scattered around inside the tent which they used as a cushion for their bed. And the straw became alight . . . but Johnny was asleep. Then, as you know, Johnny lay naked from the waist. When something cold jumped on his chest! And he sat up with a start, he wakened, he looked all around – the straw by his bedside was on fire! Johnny clasped one hand to his breast, and with the other hand he put out the fire. Then he turned around and on his hand was the frog.

'Little fella,' he said, 'you're jumping again. And you've saved my life, I could have been burnt to death only for you! Your coldness

22

wakened me. Why did you jump on me? I know why you jumped on me, you wanted to tell me the tent was on fire. And now because you've jumped, I see that yer leg must be better.' So Johnny sat up there on his bed, and he quietly unrolled the thread from the frog's leg and the matchsticks and he tested it. He found that the bone had mended completely. He said, 'Little fella, ye're all right now,' and he placed him by his bedside an went back to sleep.

In the morning when he awoke he sat up, said, 'Mary, it's time to make some tea, breakfast time.'

'Mary got up quickly, washed her face, washed her hands, made some breakfast, filled her basket, said, 'Johnny, are we staying here today?'

'No, Mary,' he said, 'I think we'll move on . . . because I see that my little friend has gone.' That's one story from my collection of 'Johnny McGill'.

The Twelve Seasons

My father told me this story years and years ago when I was wee.
I never saw it in a book or heard anyone before him telling it, but
where he'd heard it I don't know.

Many many years ago there was a woodcutter and his wife. They
lived in the forest and they had one little girl. But by sheer bad luck
the woodcutter's wife took ill and she died, left the woodcutter to
look after the small girl himself. But he tried his best, took her with
him everywhere he went, taught her whatever he knew and reared her
up the best way he could till she was about eight or nine years old.
Then he went and married again. And the woman he married had a
daughter o' her own. And he'd fetched her back with him to stay in
the house.

But the wee girl's stepmother hated her, ye know, hated her
terribly, and so did her stepsister. They made her, Mary was her
name, do everything they could get, all the work, everything. They
really despised her. If there were a bad job or a dirty job to be done,
miles to go for a message or milk or anything, Mary got the job o'
doing it. And she was a lovely little girl, and her stepsister was jealous
o' her.

But the older she began to get, the more beautiful she got, and
her father really adored her. Her mother got jealous of this, thought
that her father wasna paying enough attention to his stepdaughter. So
both o' them, the stepmother and the stepsister, made a plan that the
sooner they got rid of her the better.

So one night her father had been away in the forest. And the
next morning he told them, 'I'll not be home tonight because I've too
far to walk to cut wood. I'll stay in the forest for the night and I'll be
home tomorrow.' It was in the month of January, the winter-time,
and he says, 'The dark, it's too dark for me coming home from the
forest, so there's a little hut an I'll stay there tonight. But look after

35

Mary and see that she disna wander too far away.'

'We'll do that,' says his wife.

But about four o'clock on the winter's evening the stepmother and stepdaughter made a plan to send Mary out into the forest to see would she get lost. So she took a basket and she said, 'Here, Mary, I've a job for ye. Get yer coat and go out in the forest. Get me some strawberries because I want to make a strawberry pie! And don't come back till ye get them!'

So Mary being so kind and so tender, so nice-hearted and such a gentle little girl she just naturally takes the basket, puts on her cape (it was a cape in these days, it wasna a coat), and walks out into the forest. Away she goes wandering through the forest. Anything to please her stepmother. So she walks on and walks on, it's getting darker and darker, she wanders here and wanders there. She sits down on a log, and she starts to cry. She knows within herself that it is a hopeless case looking for strawberries in the middle o' winter.

But she looks up and sees a fire, a great big fire, a bonfire blazing in the middle o' the forest. And her feeling cold she says to herself, 'It disna matter who it is . . . it might be some nice kind person, and at least he would give me a heat at their fire. I'm awfae cold.' So she walks up to the fire, she gets near the fire. She looks, and there are twelve little men sitting round, twelve woodland elves all sitting round the fire, this great big fire.

And this one jumps up to his feet, he looks round. 'Come on, Mary,' he says, 'ye're welcome here! We've been expecting ye.' They took her in, put her sitting down beside the fire, tellt her to heat herself. They dried her cape, put it back on her.

So this one he introduces all the rest. 'Mary,' he says, 'we are the twelve months of the year, an we are woodland elves. We stay in the forest and we've been watching ye since you were very very small. But we never came near ye or never interfered. But now we see what yer stepmother's trying to do on ye, it's time we took a hand.'

'Well,' said Mary, 'my stepmother sent me into the forest to find strawberries, and I know it's hopeless searching for strawberries in the middle o' winter.'

So this one stands up and he says, 'July, this is something for you to do!'

So this wee one by the fire he stands up. He says, 'I'm July!'

So January says, 'Here, take Mary's basket and get her some strawberries. You're July, you can get strawberries.'

'Sure,' says July, 'I can get strawberries!' Away goes July.

Within seconds he is back with a lovely basket of strawberries.

'Now, says January, 'take a coal from the fire, and guide Mary back through the forest.'

And all the twelve seasons, the twelve months o' the year, bade her good-night. July led her through the forest safely back near her house shaking this coal, making a light on the path the whole way. He bade good-night to Mary and told her if she ever needed anything, always come back again.

So Mary goes, back she goes to the door. In she comes, shakes the snow off her cape. Her stepmother and her stepsister are surprised to see her. They thought she was lost and etten in the forest wi' wild animals.

So the stepmother walks and looks in the basket. She sees the lovely basket of strawberries, she snaps them out of Mary's hand, says, 'Ye got the strawberries?'

'Yes,' says Mary, 'I got the strawberries.'

So she took the strawberries and said nothing, see!

That fared very well . . . Home came Mary's daddy the next night. Mary never said anything about it. So the next night he said, 'Look, I've a lot o' work to do in the forest, an I'm going to stay away for three nights. It'll be three nights before I come back the next time.' So early in the morning he kissed wee Mary good-bye. 'Now,' he said, 'be a good girl till I come home.'

'I'll be a good girl, Daddy,' she said.

'And do everything,' he said, 'yer mummy tells ye to do.'

Away he went to his work. But Mary didna like her stepmother, because her stepmother and her stepsister didna like her.

That night just about as it was getting dark the stepmother calls for Mary again, 'Mary, I want you!'

'What is it now, Mummy?' she said.

She said, 'I want a basket of brambles, and you shall go an get them. And don't come back till ye get them!'

'Well,' says Mary, 'I'll go and try.' So away goes Mary with the basket through the forest. Now this time she knows where she's going. So she wanders on and on and on, keeps to the same path and remembers the place that July has tooken her, right down through the forest to this hollow. She sees the fire again. Up she goes. And like the first time, there sitting round the fire are the twelve months, the seasons.

So up jumps January again. 'Welcome to the fire, Mary!' he says. 'We knew you were coming. What is it this time?' says January.

'Well,' says Mary, 'it's my stepmother again.'

'And what does she want?'

'She wants a basket of brambles.'

'Ha-ha, brambles!' says January. He says, 'October, this is a job for you!'

So this wee elf that was sitting round the fire with a long white beard jumps up to his feet. 'Yes, January,' he says, 'what is it?'

He says, 'Take Mary's basket and find her a basket o' brambles!'

October comes round, catches the basket. Within seconds he's back with a beautiful basket of brambles, gives them to Mary.

'Now,' January says, 'take a coal from the fire and guide Mary back. Guide Mary back the way she came.'

But before she left, all the seasons bade her good-bye an told her, 'Mary, we won't be seeing you again, ever. But don't be afraid or don't worry, because from ever after this night you will be very happy!' And Mary bade the wee seasons, the months, good-bye.

So October takes a blazing coal from the fire as a light and guides Mary back the same way as she went, back to near her house and bids her good-bye. So she goes into her house, walks in the door, and the first thing she meets is her stepmother.

Stepmother looks at her, wonders why she has come back. 'Did ye get yer brambles?' she says.

'Yes, Mummy,' she says, 'I got the brambles.'

She looks in the basket, oh beautiful brambles! But she begins to get suspicious. Where could Mary get brambles and get strawberries in the middle o' winter? 'Mary,' she says (now she begins to talk nice to her), 'where did ye get the beautiful brambles? Tell yer mother. And where did ye get the beautiful strawberries the last night?'

Well, Mary thought a wee while. 'Mother,' she said, 'when I went into the forest I wandered searching for brambles. And I saw twelve little men, woodland elves with a fire, and they were the twelve months of the year. July asked me what I would like, an I told him I would like strawberries. Then this night October asked me what I would like, an I asked for brambles. I got brambles.'

'Oh ye foolish, foolish, foolish girl!' says the stepmother. 'I've heard of these many many years ago but never been lucky to see them. Only once in a lifetime that ever a person ever sees the twelve woodland elves! Ye should have asked for gold an diamonds! Ye would have got them.' She says, 'Daughter, get yer coat! We might

38

be in time, get yer coat, daughter! Now,' she says, 'Mary, you stay in the house and yer sister and I will go. We'll no get berries, we'll get something better than brambles. And don't leave the house till we come back!'

So away goes the stepmother and the stepsister, they put on their capes and they're away through the forest. They go back the path that Mary tellt them to take. And they see the fire, they go straight to the fire. There sitting round are the twelve woodland elves.

Up steps January, 'Welcome to the fire!' he says to the wicked mother and sister. 'What can we do for ye?'

She says, 'I want ye to give me anything I want!'

'Oh,' he says, 'we'll give ye anything ye want. What would ye like?'

She says, 'We want diamonds an pearls an gold.'

'Well,' he says, 'ye shall have it!' He said, 'March, that's something in your line, that's your job! *There are diamonds an pearls an gold – you take them where they find them!*'

And March got up. Then the wind rose, a real March hurricane, whistling wind. An a whirlwind – round and round and round both o' them – whirled them right up in the sky! Where the diamonds are the stars and the pearls and the gold of evening are, they disappeared in the distance and never was heard of again in a whirlwind!

And Mary lived on with her daddy in the wee house happy ever after, and that's the last o' the story.

Thomas
the Thatcher

I heard this story from an old man called Johnny Townsley, a cousin of my mother's. Where the story originated I don't know; it could be a German or Flemish story. Some of my forebears probably heard it when they were abroad serving in the army; this is one way a story can be passed from place to place.

Many many years ago, hundreds of years ago, when there were no police or anyone to take care of the law and one thing and the other in wee villages, a man looked after the village and they called him a 'burghmaster'. And he held court out in front of his house. If anybody had any grievances or arguments to settle they came to the burghmaster and laid their disputes before him. He settled all the arguments, he was the master of the village.

In this village, it wasnae very big, there lived an old man called Thomas and he was the thatcher. He thatched all the roofs for the people of the village and he was known far out the land as the finest thatcher in the country. And when he went and did a job it was just immaculate, nobody could beat him at his job. His name spread far and wide as 'Thomas the Thatcher' – if he had another name nobody knew it.

So one day the burghmaster is sitting at the front of his house when up comes two-three people from the village. 'Good morning, gentlemen!' he said.

'Good morning,' they said. 'Master! We have come to lay a complaint!'

'Oh aye,' he says, 'come in! Come in, sit down, men. What's yer complaint?'

'We want to lay a complaint against Thomas the Thatcher,'

40

one said.

'Come, come, come! A complaint against Thomas the Thatcher?' he said. 'I hope ye're no complaining about his work.'

'Oh no, no, no, master,' they said. 'We're no complaining about Thomas' work,' one said. 'It's not his work.'

'Well, I hope not,' said the master. 'Because he was here the day before yesterday, and look at my roof, look at my shed and the way . . . Thomas is the greatest thatcher in the world!'

'Yes,' they said, 'master, we know that. But we're here to complain about Thomas' *own* roof. The roof of his own house is in a terrible mess. And the thatch is all blown off with the wind, it's scattered high and low. It gets in wir feet, it gets in wir walks, it gets in wir gardens and he'll not do a thing about it. So we want to charge him, lay a complaint so that you will get him to sort his roof and it won't be a nuisance to us anymore!'

'Well, gentlemen,' he says, 'it's the first complaint I've ever had against Thomas the Thatcher. But it is a complaint. Thomas will be called to court tomorrow in front o' me, and I'll see his roof won't trouble you anymore. Good day, gentlemen!' Off the men go.

So the next day was court day. And Thomas was sent for, called in front of the burghmaster, and he came up along with the rest of the folk to hear the charges against him. So he sat and he heard all the charges till it would come his turn. And he was called before the burghmaster.

'Thomas,' he said, 'I have a charge against you.'

'Well, master,' he said, 'what is the charge? I have hurt no-one.'

He said, 'You have hurt no-one, but it's yer roof, Thomas. You're known as the finest thatcher in the land and ye do your work better than anyone we've ever known about. Ye work for me or work for anyone in the village. Every roof is so tidy – except yours! Why is yer roof in such a mess compared to everybody else's roof, and you are a thatcher? I want you to tell me why your roof is not like the rest of the roofs that you work on.'

So Thomas walked up. He stood in front of the master and his head was bowed. 'Master,' he said, 'it's not me. It's my friends.'

'Come, come now, Thomas,' he said, 'we're all your friends. We're all your friends here. You mean to say it's us?'

'No, no, not youse, master,' he said. 'My *little friends*,' he says, 'my friends of the air – the birds.'

'What's about the birds, Thomas?' he said. 'It's not the birds

41

that's doing it, is it?'

'No, master, it's not the birds,' he says. 'But your roof and every roof in the village is pegged down wi' ashpegs, as I did myself and made your roofs tidy and neat! But there's not one single place in your roof where a bird could lie and could sleep for the night, and keep out of the cold air, is there? I leave my roof like that for my little friends to shelter in. I could tidy up my roof and peg it down and make it beautiful like your roof or anyone else's roof, but where would my little friends go in the winter-time, master?'

The burghmaster stood up. But before he could say another word all these birds came down. And they gathered round old Thomas.

He says, 'Come, come now, children, don't cause any disturbance with the people! Ye've got a complaint against me already, I don't want any more.'

So the burghmaster stood and said, 'Thomas, you are a man, no only a thatcher but a man, a *real man*. In fact, you're the best man in this village. And I want you to know that. You go, Thomas, and take yer little friends with ye, and you leave your roof as it is and let them have shelter. We of this village never gave it a thought that a bird needs somewhere to sleep in the winter-time, we only thought of wirselves! And, gentlemen,' he said, 'if I ever hear of another complaint against Thomas the Thatcher as long as he's alive, I'll punish the complainer like I've never punished another man before in my life.' So old Thomas went away and he took his birds with him.

His roof remained like that for many's and many's a year . . . until Thomas died. And when he died the villagers built a little statue for him made of iron, metal, of an old man kneeling feeding birds. So if ever ye're somewhere in a wee village in the East and ye come across a forgotten cemetery, and ye see a statue of a rusty old man feeding birds, ye'll know that that was *Thomas the Thatcher*. And that's the end of my wee story.

Lion and
the Four Bulls

*Now the next story I'm going to tell ye is a very old story. There's
a lot o' folk tell it in different ways, ye know. But I heard this one
from my father, who told it to me a long time ago.*

There was this lion. And he was out hunting in the forest when he
spied four bulls grazing peacefully together in a corner of this little
field in the middle o' the wood. So him being an old lion, things were
very bad wi' him and he couldna catch any younger animals. He knew
fine that he wouldna be able to tackle the four bulls by himself. He
just sat down and said to himself, 'Well, I'll have to be cunning here,
I'll have to plan . . .' And like any other animal lions can be cunning
if they really try. So he raiked his brains. 'There's only one thing for
it,' he said, 'I'll just have to wait till I get one bull away from the
others a wee bit, get a wee talk to him and see what I can do. If I can
get them separated from each other, I can manage them one by one.
But I'll never manage them all together.' So he kept guard on the four
bulls, an' they kept grazing beside each other. They were the best o'
pals these four bulls, kept good company, slept beside each other at
night and grazed beside each other every day. They were good friends
these four bulls.

But anyway, the lion comes down this one morning as usual
and he spies three bulls, just the three. He says to himself, 'Now's my
chance. I wonder where the other one is?' So by sheer good luck for
the lion, bad luck for the bull, it had wandered a wee bit away from
the rest. Up goes the lion to the bull.

And the bull saw the lion coming, he just stood. He didna
worry, he wasna afraid o' him.

'Good morning,' says the lion to the bull.

43

'Good morning,' says the bull. 'Ye're far off yer hunting grounds this morning.'

'I am,' he said. 'In fact I wouldna hae been here if I hadna come to see you!'

'See me?' says the bull. 'Why should ye come an see me? Ye know, lions an bulls have always been enemies, down through the centuries.'

'Maybe so,' says the lion, 'maybe so. But anyway, I hate what's going on around here.'

'And what may that be?' says the bull.

'Well, the likes o' me,' he says, 'a lion being king o' the forest and all these things . . . I hear many things.'

'Ah, I believe that,' says the bull, 'ye hear many things.'

'But,' he says, 'things I don't like are when folk speak at other folk's back!' (As you naturally know, in these days the beasts, animals, could all speak to each other.)

'Like what?' says the bull.

'Like you an yer pals there,' he says.

'Oh,' he says, 'ye mean my mates, the other three bulls?'

'Aye.'

'Oh,' he says, 'I dinna see why they should hae much to say about anybody. We graze peacefully here, we never bother anybody.'

'Ah, but that's no the thing,' the lion says. 'Ye maybe dinna bother anybody, but what about yersels?'

'Oh,' says the bull, 'we get on fine, we, we're the best o' pals!'

'Maybe,' says the lion, 'to you, but not to other folk an the other beasts o' the jungle.'

The bull begins to think, ye see! 'Like what, Lion?' he says.

'Och well,' he says, 'a lion like me who wanders about hears a few stories here and there, and there may be nae truth into them or bits an that.'

'Well,' he says, 'What did ye hear like?'

'Well, I heard,' he said, 'the other three there, I overheard the other three the other night. And they were discussing you!'

'Me?' says the bull.

'Aye.'

He said, 'You're the oldest o' the three or the four?'

'Oh,' he says, 'I am.'

'Well,' he said, 'they were just saying a lot o' things about ye I didna like, so I thought ye would hear them!'

'Oh?' Now the bull begins to pay attention, ye see. 'What were they saying about me?' he says.

'Well they said they were just planning, the other three,' he says, 'it will soon be coming near the summer-time, an it's time youse is all splitting up. And they were thinking that you were getting too old, you couldna keep up wi' the herd, an they were thinking about turning ye out they said, an the three o' them was planning to do ye in. They said you were no more use, an ye would never manage to go out to the spring pastures an keep up wi' the rest an everything. In fact, for making calves they said you were past yer prime!'

And this made the bull very very angry. 'Well,' he said, 'I'm no very fond o' hearing the likes o' that said about me! It's no so bad if it's tellt to my face, but when it's tellt at my back . . . it's just like the three o' them, them being a wee bit younger than me. But we'll soon see about that when I go back!'

'Well,' said the lion, 'I'll be on my way. But eh, I just thought ye ought to know.'

'Well, thanks,' said the bull, 'for telling me. And eh, you being the king o' the animals I know you wouldna tell me a lie!'

'No,' says the lion. 'Well, I'll be bidding you good-day!' The lion waited till the bull walked away and he gave a wee laugh to himself. 'Now,' he says, 'the fun will start, an I'll get what I want.'

Very well, back goes the bull. The other bulls were pleased to see him, they talked to him. But he wasna very friendly to them. So he starts to the three o' them right away, and he gets on to them.

'Us?' says the three bulls. 'We never said a word about ye. In fact we were just thinking how, even how old ye are how good a fighter ye are, an what the battles ye've took us through an everything ye led. Ye led us through many's a battle against wolves and everything. We thought ye're the finest bull, ye ought to still be wir leader.'

'I don't believe ye,' says the bull, 'not one single word yese are saying! The lion wouldna tell me a lie.' And in a huff he walks away. He says, 'It'll be a while before I bother youse any more. I'll keep to mysel after this, and nobody needs to speak about me!' So he wanders away to the far-away corner o' the forest and stays by himself.

The next morning early when the other three bulls are grazing by themselves down comes Mister Lion. When the bull's back was turned to him, he jumps on the bull and kills it. He has a good feast and leaves the rest to the jackals.

So anyway the day passes by . . . he keeps his eye on the other three till he gets one o' them away from the herd. And he tells the

other one the same story, the same story. Back goes the other bull to
the other two, and he gets on to the two. And the same thing
happens: he splits up, he goes away, an naturally the lion kills him
just the same. Now there are only two bulls left.

Now these two bulls are grazing by themselves in the field.
One says to the other, 'What do ye think happened to the other two?'

'Well,' he says, 'it's up to them. They ought to know better,
that we, you and I, werena talking about them or nothing.'

'Oh well,' he says, 'maybe they're better off by theirsel, but I'll
tell ye one thing, we were a great team the four o' us. And I miss
them.'

'Well,' says the other ane, 'I dinna ken. But eh, I'm feeling
dry and I think I'll go for a drink.'

'But anyway,' he says, 'me and you hae been good pals for a
long while, an I don't think anyone will ever split us up.'

'I hope so,' says the other bull, an away he goes for a drink. So
he wanders down to the shallows for a drink, and the first thing – out
pops from the bushes – the lion.

'Well,' says the lion, 'it's a fine morning!'

'Aye,' says the bull, 'it's no a bad morning at all.'

'I see ye're down for a drink.'

'Aye.'

He said, 'Eh, what happened to the rest o' yer pals that used
to be up wi' ye? I see there's only twa o' youse there now.'

'Oh aye,' he says. 'Och, stories an tales wandering through the
forest, somebody's been telling clypes an tales. And the other two
thought they'd be better if they went on their own.'

'Oh, I believe that,' says the lion. 'But, ye ken, stories and
tales have a way o' spreading – they can be true sometimes.'

'Ah, I believe that!' says the bull.

'Anyway,' he says, 'you were just the one I was wanting to
see.'

'Me?' says the bull.

'Aye,' he says, 'it's you I was wanting to see. Eh, I was just
wanting to tell ye something I think ye ought to hear.'

'Like what?' says the bull.

'Well, I just overheard yer mate,' he says, 'the other day saying
an awfae things about ye.'

'Me?' says the bull.

'Aye,' he says, 'you – just saying how –'

'Like what?' says the bull.

46

'Well,' the lion said, 'he said you were too young, you werena able to keep up wi' them and you were a poor fighter. And when any fights took place against wolves or animals ye always made sure that ye were away behind the rest and ye were never touched. And ye havenae got a scratch nor nothing to show for it – in all yer years!'

This made the bull very very angry and he said, 'He did say that about me?'

'That's what he said,' the lion said, 'an me being the king o' the forest I dinna like to hear naebody spoken about! So I thought ye ought to ken.'

'Well,' says the bull, 'we'll see about that, if I'm feart or no!' So back he goes. And he challenges the other bull to a fight.

The other bull said, 'I never said a word about ye, I never spoke about ye! Somebody's been telling ye clypes an tales.'

But he was so angry that he says, 'Look, I think it's the best thing that me and you should part company. I still believe the lion – the lion wouldna tell me any tales!'

'Well,' says the bull, 'if that's what ye think ye can be on yer way! I've nae more need for yer company!'

So away he goes. And the next day the lion kills him. Till there's only one bull left. And he's wandering around grazing by himself, when out pops the lion and kills him. So after this was finished the lion says, 'Well, that's my job done! I got the four o' them an I enjoyed myself wi' these four. But they listened to me, but one thing they should have known: *there's always safety in numbers.*' And that's the last o' the story!

The Princess
and the Fox

*This is a very old fairy tale that was told and passed among the
travelling people of the West Coast for many hundreds of years. I
heard it when I was fourteen from old 'Bonnie Duncan' of
Kintyre, my uncle. The travellers had a way of putting their stories
together which is a lot different from the folk who wrote fairy
tales; so this traveller tale is very strange.*

When Alden, the son of the fairy queen, was being forced to marry
a princess he did not love he was very upset. His mother had coaxed
him to marry a distant princess in fairyland, but he did not love her
in any way. And his mother prigged and preached, 'Alden, she is a
beautiful woman. You must marry her, she is a friend of the family!'

He said, 'Mother, I know what would make you happy would
make me unhappy!'

'But,' she says, 'I've made arrangements for the wedding and it
will begin in a short time.'

He says, 'Mother, not without my permission!'

She said, 'Alden, my son, your father would be proud of you
to marry a friend of the family.'

But Alden was not happy. He wandered away to be by himself
thinking about what he was going to do. He travelled all day long till
he came round fairyland. He saw a long dark tunnel, and he said to
himself, 'I have never been here before. Where does this lead to?' He
walked and he walked through the tunnel . . . it was very dark. So he
travelled on always thinking, behind him was the worry he was going
to marry someone he did not love. And then he saw the light ahead in
front of him. 'At last,' he said, 'it's leading somewhere.' Travelling on
he came through the tunnel, and there was bright sunlight. There was
a beautiful hillside which he had never seen before in his life. He was

48

thirsty. And then he saw a beautiful well. Alden said, 'Where is this place? Where have I come to? This is not fairyland.' He didn't realize he was on the land of the mortals. He had travelled through the tunnel from fairyland to earth, a place he had never been before. And then, because he was thirsty, he bent down at the well to have a drink.

But lo and behold he did not know that a shepherd's daughter, Mary, had come to the well to drink. She was tending her father's sheep on the hillside, and to her this was the Fairy Well – called the Fairy Well because people long before her had said that fairies sometimes came to drink there. She'd heard these stories, she believed and she always came to drink at this well when she was thirsty tending her father's sheep – believing someday she would see a fairy. But Alden knew nothing about this.

So she was tired and the sun was shining and it was a very warm day. It was a beautiful well out on the hillside and the water was crystal clear. Mary, with her bare feet, left her shepherd's crook beside her. She bent down on her knees to have a drink. And she drank from the well. And she looked – there before her stood the most beautiful young man she'd ever seen in her lifetime. He was a fairy. She stood aghast as she looked – he was beautiful but so small. She said, 'A-A-Are you really a fairy?'

And Alden stood there, he was as surprised as she was, and he said, 'Yes, I am.'

And she said, 'Where do you come from?'

He said, 'I come from fairyland.'

'Well,' she said, 'I've heard stories of the Fairy Well. But I have never seen a fairy before in my life.' She stared at him and he stared at her. She said to him, 'What is your name?'

He said, 'My name is Alden. I am the son of the Queen of Fairyland. And she wants me to get married to someone I don't love.'

Mary was tall by him and still on her knees drinking by the well. She said, 'You are a handsome young man.'

'Well . . . and you are a handsome young woman, though you're taller than me,' he said.

She said, 'I wish I was like you.'

And when Alden looked at her she was so beautiful in his eyes. He said, 'Look, would you like to be like me?'

She said, 'I would love to be like you.'

And Alden had the powers from his mother. So then he stretched out his hand and took her hand in his. And he held on to her hand; slowly as he squeezed her hand she began to come smaller and

49

smaller and smaller and smaller . . . till she was his size.

She said, 'What did you do to me?'

He said, 'Would you like to come with me to fairyland?'

She said, 'I would love to come with you to fairyland.'

'Well,' he said, 'now you're my size why don't you come with me?' So he took her and he led her back through the tunnel.

And Mary was gone . . . her father waited and he waited and he waited, but she never returned. The sheep spread far across the hillside, but she was gone. Alden took her back to fairyland and took her to his mother's palace.

He said, 'Mother, you have been wanting me to get married.'

She says, 'Who is that you have with you? That's not one of us.'

He says, 'No, Mother. It is a mortal. It is a human from earth, and I'm in love, I want to marry her – her I want for my wife.'

'Alden,' she says, 'it will never happen! It will cause trouble. It never could be.'

He says, 'Look, if I don't get her, Mother, I won't have anyone.' So he finally convinced his mother he would have her and nothing else.

Then his mother relented and a great wedding was held in fairyland. And Mary and Alden were married. They settled down with their mother, who was an old woman, the Queen of Fairyland. And a few years passed by. They had a little baby girl, the most beautiful little girl you ever saw in your life. They called her 'Sunlight'. And the old grandmother loved her and Alden and Mary loved her like nothing on this earth. She was the most beautiful child, but she was half mortal.

But after a few more years and as the days passed by, Alden saw that his wife Mary had gotten very sad. One day Alden turned to her and said, 'You know, some day when my mother is gone I will become king and you will become queen.'

She said, 'I don't want to be Queen of Fairyland.'

He said, 'What is troubling you?'

She said, 'I would love to see earth again. I don't want to become queen, I just want to see my beautiful earth.'

'Well,' he said, 'my dear, if that makes you happy I will take you to see your beautiful earth again!'

So he took his little daughter and left her with his mother. And he took Mary by the hand and they travelled through the tunnel of darkness once more to the well, where she had longed to be, where he had first met her. Alden's mother waited and she waited and she waited for a long long time, but Mary and Alden never returned. The old queen was very sad to lose her son and her daughter-in-law, even though she didn't like her very much. But years passed by and the beautiful little princess she grew up.

Now the queen she began to get very old, and she knew some day she was going to die. And there was no-one to rule fairyland but the daughter of Alden. One day she called her before her. She said, 'Sunlight, you know someday you'll have to become Queen of Fairyland. But you're *ugly* – not ugly as a person, you're the most beautiful person in fairyland. But you're ugly because you're half mortal. There's no way you can ever become Queen of Fairyland – first you'll have to kiss your land good-bye. *You must go out to the earth and meet a mortal, and kiss him good-bye for ever before you can become queen.*' By this time the queen was very ill, very sick, she was dying.

And she said, 'Grandmother, when must I go?'

She says, 'As soon as you want to. But you must kiss or be kissed by a mortal before you return! Your father is gone and your mother is gone, they have never returned. You must travel through the tunnel of darkness and there you will come to the earth, the land of the mortals. There you will find a well and there you will stay till you meet a mortal. And you must kiss or be kissed by a mortal before you return to fairyland! Then you will be a *beautiful* princess, and then you will become the Queen of Fairyland!'

So the little Sunlight she set off on her journey and she travelled the road her father had years before. She travelled through the tunnel of darkness and she came to the land of brightness. There she found the earth and there she came to the well. She sat by the well and she drank by the well, and lo and behold at that very moment who should come to the well for a drink but a young fox! He had come to drink because he was thirsty.

And when he leaned over and started lapping the water, he looked. There stood before him a little, beautiful princess.

And the princess looked up when she saw the fox and she said, 'Oh-h-h, at last! You are a mortal! I have found you . . . my granny said I must kiss you. Talk to me, mortal, please, kiss me!'

But the poor little fox he stood there and he saw the most beautiful thing he had ever seen in his life, a princess from fairyland. And the little fox was so excited he could not speak to her.

She says, 'Please talk to me, talk to me, please! Kiss me please, so I can go home.'

But the fox couldna speak to her.

She says, 'Well, I'll kiss you then.' So the princess she leaned over and she kissed the wee fox on the side of his cheek. And he stood there. She said, 'Good-bye, mortal, now I can go home to fairyland and tell my grandmother I have kissed a mortal.' So she made her way once again through the tunnel of darkness back to fairyland. And she came up to her grandmother, who was lying in bed very sick.

She said, 'Sunlight, you have returned!'

'Yes, Grandmother,' she said, 'I have come back.'

She said, 'Did ye go to the land of the mortals?'

'I did, Grandmother,' she says.

And she says, 'Did ye see a mortal? Did ye kiss a mortal?'

'I did, Grandmother,' she said.

'And what did it look like?'

'Oh,' she said, 'he had two long ears and he had a beautiful long face and he had a beautiful tail.'

And her grandmother says, 'Ye know, girl, that was not a mortal ye saw . . .'

'It must be a mortal, Grandmother,' she said, 'he was the only one at the well!'

She said, 'That was a fox! You will have to go back again.'

'Oh, Grandmother,' she said, 'I thought it was a mortal.'

'You will have to go back again.'

Now the fox when the little Sunlight had gone stood there by the well. He was transformed, he was in love. He had seen the most beautiful thing in his life. But he could not speak, he could not talk. And he sat there . . . he was in love.

And lo and behold far away from the well by the village lived Jack with his mother. And Jack had stayed with his mother for many years. Jack worked around his mother's croft and worked hard. But because they lived on the hillside they had a shortage of water. And one day the well by their croft had gone dry, they had no water.

And Jack's mother turned to him. She said, 'Jack, we must have water because I cannot cook.'

'But, Mother,' he said, 'the well has gone dry.'

She says, 'Jack, I must have a drink of clear clean water.'

'Well,' he said, 'Mother, I'll go and fetch ye some.'

'I'll tell ye where ye'll find water, Jack,' she says. 'You go to the Fairy Well on the hillside. There is the most beautiful water of all.'

'Where do I find it, Mother?' he said.

So she gave him directions. Jack took a big milk-can that his mother used to milk the cows and he walked through the hillside from the directions his mother gave him to the Fairy Well, where he'd never been before. And when he came up to the Fairy Well from his mother's directions, the first thing he saw was the beautiful sparkling water. And sitting beside the well was a little fox. Jack ducked in the can and he filled it and he took a drink himself. But he looked and he saw the fox sitting there. He said, 'Little creature, what's the trouble? What's wrong with ye? Are ye sick, are ye ill?'

But the fox never moved. The fox was in love.

Jack said, 'Ye're sick, ye're ill!' Now Jack liked all the little creatures and he'd mended many, and to see a puir little fox sitting by the well he felt sad for it. So he filled his can and he took the fox under his arm, he carried it. It never moved, it was just in a kind of a trance. He carried the fox back with him and he brought back the large milk-can full of water to his mother.

And his mother was surprised when she saw him coming back. She said, 'Jack, what have you got there?'

He says, 'Mother, I got to the well as you see. It's a beautiful well and I've brung back the water for ye. But Mother, I found a wee fox by the well and it's sick, there's something wrong with it. I've never seen one in such a state – it's kind of petrified.' And he set it down by the fire. He coaxed it with something to eat, he coaxed it with something to drink but the wee fox just sat there and it wouldna move. And he kindled up the fire, his mother made him something to eat. And the fox just sat by the fireside. 'Mother,' he said, 'what do you think's wrong with it?'

She said, 'I dinna ken, Jack, what's wrong with it.'

And then as it sat by the fireside Jack looked: he saw a big tear coming down the fox's eye. And the tear stopped on the fox's cheek, it reflected like a mirror – and in the tear Jack saw the face of the most beautiful princess he ever saw in his life. He says, 'Mother, look! Do you see what I see?' And the tear dropped on the floor.

She says, 'What do you see, Jack?'

'Mother, did you see what happened?' He says, 'I saw the face of the most beautiful creature in the world falling from the eye of the fox!'

'Well,' she says, 'Jack, he must have seen it at the well. Take him back to the well, Jack, and leave him.'

'But, Mother,' he says, 'how can *I* see anything at the well?'

She says, '*Jack, my grandmother tellt me if you want to see something that you cannot see, all ye have to do is take a handful of rowans and suck them, and then ye'll have superior powers.*'

53

'Well,' Jack said, 'Mother, I'll take the fox back to the well.' So Jack took the fox under his arm and he walked back to the well – but passing by on his road there was a mountain ash and it was hanging with rowans. So Jack took a handful of rowans and he started putting them in his mouth, *and they were bitter.* But he sucked them and swallowed the juice, and he walked on till he came to the well. He left the little fox at the well.

Now, the old queen in fairyland had turned to the princess and said, 'Look, Sunlight, you must again go back to the well!'

But when Jack places the wee fox by the well, the wee fox takes one look . . . and it was gone. And Jack stood there. He said, 'I wonder what was wrong with the little fella?' But he watched the fox disappear in the mountain very slowly, it wandered away through the hillside. And Jack sat there by the well with a handful of rowans. Sucking the rowans, he said, 'If the fox saw it, I must!'

Sunlight had left fairyland again for the second time, and travelled through the tunnel of darkness the way her father had and retraced her father's footsteps of a long time ago. She came to the well.

Then Jack was leaning down to drink when he looked – and he saw the most beautiful creature he'd ever seen in his lifetime. He was on his knees drinking when she appeared before him.

And she said, 'Are you a mortal? Are you a human?'

'Of course,' says Jack, 'I'm a human. I saw you before.'

She says, 'You never saw me before.'

He said, 'Yes, I've seen you in a fox's teardrop.'

'Oh-h-h, so my granny told me! She said I'd made a big mistake. But are you a human?'

Jack said, 'I am a human.'

She said, 'Will you kiss me, human, so I can return once more to fairyland?'

And Jack said, 'You are the most beautiful creature I've ever seen in my life.' And he leaned over and he kissed the little princess on the cheek.

She said, 'Thank you!' and she walked away and was gone.

Jack stood there dumbfounded. And he never felt like this before in his life. He said, 'I have never seen anything so beautiful. No wonder the fox was in love! And so am I.' But he looked all around . . . The well was bubbling, the water was bright, but the little princess was gone. Jack walked home to his mother with a wonderful feeling of love in his heart, *and a bitter bitter taste in his mouth from the rowan berries.* And that is the end o' my story.

The Boy
and the Snake

*There are many beautiful stories on the West Coast of Scotland,
but the most beautiful, the most wonderful story of all I think is
kind of sad. This story was told to me by an old crofting man who
had it told to him when he was a child by his grandfather. I hope
you will like it. It tells you that parents think they know what is
best for their children, but sometimes the children know better, so
listen to this little story.*

Away back in the West Coast where I come from there's an old
derelict farm building, and it's out on the hillside. It is ruins now and
has been for many years, for over a hundred and fifty years. It all
started with a shepherd and his family, his wife and his little boy.
This shepherd had a little sheep farm on the hillside and he had many
sheep. And he had a little boy called Iain. Because Iain was so young,
just about five years old, and because it was so far to the village, Iain
couldn't go to school. His daddy said, 'When you get a little older I
will buy you a pony. Then you can ride the five miles to school. But
in the meantime you must stay with your mother, help your mother
around the house with her work while I tend my sheep.' Iain was a
very happy little boy. There was no-one more beautiful and happier
than him. And he played around the farm all day. He had plenty
pets – dogs, cats, geese, hens – but he paid no attention to them.

But one summer's morning his father was out hunting the
sheep as usual, when he fell over a rock and he hurt his leg. He
barely managed to walk home. Now he could not tend his sheep.

So Iain would always come downstairs in the morning to the
kitchen table, and his mother would give him a plate of porridge and
milk for breakfast. Then he would take the plate and walk out the

55

door, walk away up the hillside, among the heather . . . There Iain came to a large rock on the hillside. He took the spoon and he halft the porridge down the centre, put one half to that side o' the plate and the other half to the other side of the plate. Then he 'tap, tap, tapped' on the rock with his spoon. And from out behind the rock came a large adder, a poisonous snake – there are many on the hills in the West Coast. The snake came to his plate. It started to eat the porridge off the one side of the plate, and Iain ate from the other side. If the snake dared cross to his side of the plate he tapped it with his spoon, and it pulled its head back. 'Stay on your own side!' Iain would say. Every morning he would go out and do this.

But this one morning the father said to his wife, 'Why does Iain go outside with his porridge? Why doesn't he take it at the table?'

She said, 'Husband, he's not doing any harm. He's a bright little boy an he just goes out . . . he likes to eat it by himself.'

So his daddy having a sore leg said, 'Well, why doesn't he stay here with us? I like my son to have his breakfast with me. Where does he go anyhow with his porridge?'

And his wife said, 'He just goes out an eats it out on the hillside, he loves doing it outside.'

'Well, why doesn't he stay and have it at the table? I want my boy to stay and eat porridge with me at the table!'

But the next morning, as usual, Iain comes downstairs, gets his plate of porridge and walks outside with it. And his daddy's leg is beginning to get a little better by this time. He takes a walking stick from behind the door and he hobbles after Iain keeping a little distance behind him, among the heather. He watches Iain going to the rock. He watches Iain taking the spoon and halfing the porridge in two; and he watches him 'tap, tap, tapping' on the rock with his spoon. He watches the snake coming out . . . he is terrified. He has seen so many snakes on the hill in his time hunting sheep, but he has never seen one as large as this! This one is over four feet long. Iain's father is terrified. It comes up to the plate, it starts to eat the porridge. And when it finishes its side it tries to cross the plate, an Iain hits it with the spoon – it pulls its head back!

He quickly hobbled back home to his wife and he said, 'Do you know what your son is doing? He's out there, in the hillside, an he's eating with a snake, a poisonous adder! And to make matters worse he hits it with his spoon! If that snake bites him he shall die!'

'Well,' she said, 'husband, he's been doing that all summer long, and if that snake was going to bite him it would have done so a

56

long time ago. I think ye should leave him alone.'

'I'm not having my son eating with a snake, I'm not having my son eating with a snake! That terrible adder,' he said, 'that's a poisonous adder. Tomorrow morning when he comes downstairs for his breakfast you send him up to tidy up his bedroom, an I'll take the porridge to the snake!'

So sure enough, next morning Iain comes downstairs and he says, 'Could I have my breakfast, Mummy?'

She says, 'After you tidy up your room. It's in a terrible mess, your bedroom. Collect your toys and tidy up for your mummy!'

'Yes, Mummy!' And he ran up the stairs, he went to his room. While he was gone his daddy took the empty plate and spoon, and he hobbled out of the kitchen. He took his gun from behind the door and he walked . . . to the stone. He 'tap, tapped' on the rock with his spoon. Out came the snake, and he shot the snake. He carried it back to the house. He buried it in the garden. Iain knew nothing of this. He was busy working in his room. His father came in and sat down at the table.

Sure enough, soon Iain comes downstairs once more. He says, 'Mummy, can I have my breakfast, please?' And his mother gives him a plate of porridge and milk and his spoon. He hurriedly – happy little boy – walks away through his little path through the heather.

His father turns round to his wife and says, 'He's in for a big surprise when he goes back. I shot the snake.'

'Well,' she said, 'I don't think you should have done that.'

Iain goes to the rock once more with his spoon, and he halfs the porridge in two as usual – one side to that side, one side to the other side o' the plate – then 'tap, tap, tap' on the rock. And he waits.

No answer.

He taps again with his spoon.

No answer.

Three times he taps. No snake. He says, 'Well, my pet, you seem to not be hungry this morning.' And he lifts the plate, porridge and all, he walks back with it. He puts it on the table.

His mummy says, 'What's the trouble, Iain? Are ye, are ye not having yer breakfast this morning?'

He says, 'I don't feel very hungry.' He walks up to his bedroom.

The next morning he went with his porridge to the stone. The same thing happened. He went with it for three times. Nothing happened. On the fourth day Iain did not come downstairs.

By this time his daddy's leg is better. He says, 'What's the trouble? Where is Iain this morning?' He goes up to get Iain.

Iain is just lying in bed staring at the ceiling. He would not talk to his father in any way. Nor he would not talk to his mother in any way. He just lay there. He completely lost the will to live, in any way. He lay there for nearly a week without food or drink.

His father said, 'This cannot go on.' So he took his pony, he rode down to the little village and brought back the doctor.

The doctor came in and asked the trouble. They told him, but they never mentioned the snake. The doctor went up to Iain's bedroom, he examined him in every way. He could find nothing wrong with him. But Iain wouldn't even talk to the doctor, he just lay staring into space. Then the doctor came down and he said to Iain's mother and father, 'I can't seem to see anything wrong with yer son. He just seems to have lost the will to live. Has anything happened to upset him in any way?'

And it was Iain's mother who said, 'Prob'ly it was the snake.'

The doctor said, 'Snake? What snake? Tell me about it.'

Iain's father told the doctor about the snake he had shot.

The doctor was very upset. He said, 'Ye know, children are very queer sometimes, and they love to choose their own pets in their own time.' And he said, 'I'm sorry, ye should not have touched the snake. I don't think it would ever have touched him in any way. How long had he been feeding this snake?'

She said, 'He'd been doing this since the beginning of summer, an the summer before that when he was only four. I never knew anything about the snake. But he was a quite happy child, an I just let him take his breakfast outside every morning,' said his mother.

'Well,' the doctor said, 'I think you've made a grave mistake. I'll come back and see him again, but I don't think there's very much I can do for yer son. He'll have to come out of it himself.'

But Iain lay in bed and he just pined away. He finally died.

And his mother and father were so upset, they sold the farm and moved off to another part of the country. The funny thing was, no-one seemed to want the farm after the story spread from the doctor. The farm stood there till it became a ruins. But Iain's daddy never forgave himself for shooting the queerest pet that any child could have – a poisonous snake.

And that, children, is a true story that happened a long time ago on the West Coast of Scotland. If you were there with me today I could lead you to the same place, to the ruins of the farmhouse; I've passed it many times on my travels through the West Coast.

58

House of the
Seven Boulders

*This story was told to me a long time ago by an old cousin of my
father's called Willie Williamson. God rest his soul, he died when
he was ninety years old in the old people's home in Cambeltown,
Argyll. And this was one of his favourite stories. It is a legend, it
happened a long long time ago.*

Away in the West Coast there is a ruins of a great house. And today
it is known as the House of the Seven Boulders, but in bygone times
it was not known by this name . . . Because in this great house there
lived an old woman who was said to have magical powers, and she
had seven great warrior sons. They raided far across the land, stole
and robbed, and everyone was powerless against these sons of hers.
The king soon got tired of them raiding across the land. He sent
armies to try and capture them, but they were great warrior
swordsmen – no less than giants these men! His army would return
bloody and battered from having a battle because they had to pass
through a narrow gorge that led to the great house where they lived.
And when these seven brothers held that pass no-one could ever get
through, and there was no way to the house except through this
narrow pass. There they lived with their mother, and from there they
raided far and wide. The king had tried many many times to capture
these great brothers, but without success! He offered a large reward to
anyone who could rid him of the warriors who raided across his lands,
but no-one could do anything to beat these brothers.

Now the king had one daughter who was a young maiden of
only eighteen years old. And she saw that her daddy was upset when
word came again to his palace, the warriors had been out once more
raiding. She saw that there was no way her daddy was going to get

59

help of any description from anyone. So one evening she turned to him and said, 'Father, why don't you let me help you against these great warriors?'

He says, 'You, my dear? And what could you do against these warriors? I've sent my armies, I've sent troops and they've returned beaten and bloody and battered. I've offered a large ransom to anyone who could help me. And no-one seems to help me. What could you do?'

'Please, Father,' she said, 'let me go! There must be something I can do.'

He said, 'My dear, I love you! You're my only daughter. There's no way in the world I'm going to let you out of my sight – never mind let you go up where there live these great warriors!'

She says, 'Please, Father, I can help, I know I can help!'

Well, the king finally considered this for a long time . . . he'd do anything to get rid of these warrior swordsmen. He said, 'How would you go about it?'

'Well,' she says, 'I would need help.'

'Well,' he says, 'there's no help I can give you!'

She says, 'Father, I don't want any help from you. I'll go and see my friend – the old henwife – she will help me.'

Now not far from the palace there lived an old woman who was a henwife. And she too was known to have magical powers. She was a great friend of the princess, ever since she was a child. And the princess had visited her many times. So this day she took off to visit the old henwife, and she explained to her what she wanted to do.

And the old henwife was very sad to hear her mention that she would even try and go and do something about these warriors. She said, 'My dear, what can ye do? There's nothing really ye can do.'

She says, 'Please, mother,' as she called the old henwife, 'help me! You're the only one . . . my father is upset and he just can't go on like this. He's so unhappy when he hears word of these men raiding across his land, across his kingdom.'

'Well,' says the old woman, 'there's only one thing I could do. I can't really help you to get rid of the warriors, but I can tell ye what to do.' She said, 'Look, you know what a *goose-girl* is?'

And the princess said, 'Yes, I've heard of goose-girls.'

'Well,' she says, 'Look, I'll dress you as a goose-girl and I'll give ye some geese. Then you make your way to the home of the warriors, and there you'll be on yer own. Because they tell me their mother is a very kindly soul, even though they say she has magical

60

powers. And maybe she will help you.'

So it was arranged that the next day the princess would dress herself as a goose-girl, with her bare feet and a ragged dress and her stave. She would drive some geese across the land till she came to the gorge that led to the home of the great warriors. The young princess told her father the plan she had in mind. And he was very upset. He thought in his mind he would never see his little daughter again – if she was captured by the great warriors.

But she said, 'Father, have no fear, I'll be able to take care of myself.'

So the very next day the young princess said good-bye to her father. She dressed herself as a goose-girl in a ragged dress and plaited her hair in two plaits down her back. With her stick and her twelve geese she set off across the land. She travelled for many days, doing her best, as the old henwife had told her, to sell some geese and swap some geese, to give away a female and receive a male goose from people along the roadway. Till finally she made her way to the narrow pass that led to the home of the great warriors, to the great house. And there she walked through the pass driving her geese, and no-one stopped her. Till she came to the great house, and her geese began to eat round the front of the house. And she went up to the great house and she knocked on the door.

Lo and behold it was opened by a tall old woman – she had never seen a woman so tall in her lifetime – the old woman herself was nearly seven feet tall! And she bended down and she said, 'Little one, what are ye doing here?'

And the princess said, 'Ma'm, I'm just a goose-girl, and I was wondering if ye're needing any geese?'

'Oh,' she said, 'needing any geese, my dear! I don't need any geese. My sons bring me everything I need. But if they find you here yer life is in danger.'

She says, 'Please help me, I'm hungry and tired.'

So the old woman said, 'The first thing we have to do . . .' The old woman was glad to have female company because she'd spent her life by herself and had never seen a human being like her, a woman like herself or a girl for many many years. She only lived her life with these great sons of hers. And she was happy to see the young girl. She says, 'First we must shut up yer geese where my sons won't find them. They'll be home shortly.' So she locked the geese up in a little shed and she said, 'Come with me!'

And she led the young girl into the great house, there sat her

61

down and gave her something to eat. 'Now,' she said, 'my dear, if my sons return and find you here you'll be in terrible trouble.' And then she heard the clashing of swords and the tramping of feet. She said, 'They're coming home!' And she shut her in a small cupboard in the great hall. There the young princess sat in terror in the great hall in the cupboard.

Then in walked these great seven sons of the old woman and arranged themselves along the great dining hall – and demanded their mother to feed them and bring them wine! So the old mother fed them and brought them great flagons of wine. And then they sat and drank and talked and boasted about their escapades across the land.

Then . . . the young girl sneezed with the dust in the cupboard!

And the oldest brother he rose and said, 'Mother, you've been deceiving us, there's someone here!' And he ran to the cupboard, he opened it and there stood the young goose-girl, the princess. He put his hand in and he pulled her out. He said, 'Brothers, look what I have found!' And he brought her forth. He said to his mother, 'Where did she come from?'

And the mother said, 'It's only a goose-girl, leave her alone!'

He said, 'A goose-girl here or a goose-girl there – she's a young handsome woman! And one of us must have her!'

The seven brothers started passing the young princess from each to the other, all demanding that *he* wanted her! And the old woman could not take this.

She ran from the great dining hall out to the front door of the house. Then she clapped her hands and cried, 'Bring your swords, we're gettin invaded!'

And the seven brothers grabbed their swords and ran out the front door to see who was invading them!

And the young princess sat in terror.

Then there was quietness . . .

And the old woman walked in and she said, 'My little dear, you can come up now.' The young princess was sitting on the floor. 'You can come up now, my dear, everything's all right. They'll never bother you again.'

The young girl said, 'Where have they gone, mother?'

She says, 'Come with me and I'll show you. They'll never trouble you or anyone again.' And she led the princess to the great front door. There before the door stood *seven great boulders*, each one weighing over three ton, right beside the door of the house.

She turned to the little goose-girl. 'I know why you came here, my dear . . . you are not a goose-girl. You are the daughter of the king, you are a princess! And you have come to rid the land of my sons. Well,' she says, 'it was time the world was rid of them, not just the land. Because they've been causing too much trouble, and I would never let them harm you.'

And the young princess said to the old woman, 'Yes, I am the princess, mother. I came to try and help my father the king to rid the land of these great warriors of yours.'

The old woman said, 'Well, my dear, you can go home to your father now and tell your father they will never bother him again, because they are gone.'

And the princess said, 'The only way I'll go back, mother – if you will come with me and be my companion for the rest of my life.' Because she wasn't really a very old woman.

So the next day the little princess and the old woman said good-bye to the great house and walked away to her father's kingdom. And the king was happy to hear that the great warriors were gone for ever. And the princess had a great companion. But as years passed by the house became derelict . . . The roof fell in and the walls began to fall down. The House of the Seven Boulders became overgrown with grass and trees and thorns and branches. And it came to pass that people could no more explain why anyone would have seven large boulders at the very door of their house . . . But these were the seven great warrior sons who were transformed to stones by their own mother. That is a legend, that is true.

Seal Mother

*In my youth I had not spent very much time among the travellers
of Kintyre (the westernmost peninsula of the Scottish West
Highlands and the ancestral home of my parents), but I spent some
time with my father's two sisters Rachel and Nellie in Tarbert on
Loch Fyneside. They stayed in a camp, a large traveller-made
tent, in a wee field surrounded by rhododendron by the sea. When
my Aunt Rachel told me this silkie tale, about seal-folk who are
half human and half seal, I think I would have been fourteen,
shortly after I'd left school. It was a summer's evening. So we
were sitting inside the tent. And that's what Aunt Rachel used to
always do in the evening – comb her hair. She had the most
beautiful hair, so long she could sit on it and the colour of newcut
corn, pure yellow. She wasn't very old at that time, about
thirty-eight; she'd never married. I said, 'Aunt Rachel, you've got
beautiful hair, it's the most beautiful hair I ever saw in my life.
My Aunt Nellie has lovely hair too, but hers is grey.' So she
turned round and said to me, 'Brother,' (she called all her nephews
'brother') 'I'll tell ye a wee story. This has got to do wi' hair –
seeing you brought up the subject.' So I'm going to tell you this
story the way my Aunt Rachel told it to me. I hope you'll like it.*

Many years ago away in the West Coast there lived a widow-woman
and she had two beautiful daughters. Their father had been a
fisherman and was drowned in an accident at sea, and the widow
reared these two girls by herself. One's name was June and the other's
name was May, called after the months they were born. This widow
was the nicest person that ever walked this earth. She was respected
and loved by the people in the village; it was a small village away
from the shore a wee bit. She stayed by the seaside in a cottage that
had been owned by her husband's father long before her time. And
her two daughters attended the village school. But there was nothing

in the world the widow wouldn't do to help anybody out in any circumstances – nothing was too hard for her. The most amazing thing about her was her hair – even though she was up in her mid-fifties it was a mass of golden curls right down her back. Everyone admired it and said it was the most beautiful they had ever seen.

The oldest daughter June, a year older than May, was just like her mother in every way. Quiet, kindly, good-hearted, she would help anybody out in any circumstances. She loved her mother and when asked to do something she never spoke a single word back. But as June was good May was wicked. She would do nothing for her mother. May was even hated by her school mates. They were pleased when she came fourteen, that she left the school. But both girls, one after the other left the school and stayed with their mother.

At the front of the cottage on the shoreside where they lived was a small island, about five or six acres of rocks and stones. When the tide went out there was a small strand, a bay of sand you could walk over to the island. The bay was famed for its cockles, and round it the mother used to send the girls to gather the seafood they loved to eat. But whenever the girls went to the island all May wanted was to go and torment the wee animals. In the summer-time she would go where the gulls were laying on the shoreside, break their eggs and throw them in the water. And then when she came to a nest with wee baby gulls she would catch them, put them in the sea to see if they would swim – it was horrible – they were just newly out of their eggs! And June would come back complaining to her mother.

But her mother was such a kindly person she never took sides, never said a word, just 'Leave May alone, someday she'll repent for her wickedness, June, you watch my words.' Now the mother was a great knitter, she earned her living making jerseys, sweaters and cardigans. If she felt sorry for somebody, though they only gave her half price for a sweater, she would give it to them. So she would sit by the fireside knitting day out and day in. But at night-time she used to sit and let June comb her hair, the most beautiful golden hair you ever saw in your life. June wasn't her favourite, she never made fish of one or flesh of the other. But May would never take a turn at combing her mother's hair. She could always find some devilment to do instead. And May was never scolded.

Then one day the mother said to June, 'The tide is out. Will ye go and gather Mummy some cockles? Ask May if she'll go along with ye.'

And June in her bare feet took the basket, said, 'May, Mummy says we must go and gather cockles.'

'Well, I'll come with you but I'm not going to help,' she said. So away they went. The mother looked out, saw the girls going. June carried the basket and May just splashed her feet across the water, walked with her head in the air doing nothing! The mother shook her head and sat down, started knitting again. By the time she'd finished the two girls had come back, and June had a full basket of cockles.

June placed it down beside her mother. 'Mummy! May has been horrible today, really horrible. She never helped me, Mummy, in no way. When she came to the beach she picked up cockles and smashed them against the stones. She tormented a poor starfish and with a stick poked holes in a jellyfish washed up by the tide. Then she pulled the legs off three or four crabs, Mother, and turned them on their backs for the sun to get them. Mother, I just can't go on any longer with this, you'll have to do something about her! I know she's my sister, but why can't she be like you and me? Why can't she love these little creatures?'

The mother said, 'June, it's about time that she was taught a lesson.' That's all she said.

So naturally they had their supper and sure enough June said, 'Mummy, I want to brush your hair.' June started to brush her mummy's hair and May went out to the shed where they had some hens for eggs. She started poking the hens with sticks, pulling their feathers, aggravating them in the shed.

The mother turned to June, 'Where is May?'

'Oh,' she said, 'you know, Mother, where she'll be – out tormenting the hens again!'

'Well,' she said, 'June, I think the time has come . . .'

'But Mother,' she said, 'we don't want to hurt her in any way.'

'Oh no,' she said, 'I'll no hurt your sister, you believe it. Not in any way!'

It was about the middle of summer, the month of July. And there were great tides. Sometimes during these heavy tides the small island across from where they stayed got completely bare, except for a part at the end where it was deep and full of rocks. So this one morning May got up and saw the tide was out as far as she could see across the strand. She hurried, had her breakfast, ran out to the beach. Her mother and June watched.

'There she goes, Mother,' June said. 'That's her on her way

again. There's many a crab will lose its legs and many a jellyfish will be full o' holes before night-time, Mother, before the tide comes in. Mother, I'm really sorry!'

'Never mind, June,' she said. 'You go and tidy up yer bedroom.' And June went away to do her mother's bidding.

When June had walked into her bedroom and closed the door, the mother went and took down her sealskin coat that always hung behind the door. She put the coat over her shoulders, put her arms in it and walked away along the beach. Now by this time May had landed on the island that was covered in rocks and stones. People could disappear on it, and there was a big beach. May walked along it.

The mother walked along the shore till she came to a part where it was so deep the tide never went out very far; it was a heap of large rocks. She went behind one, pulled her sealskin coat up round her neck, sat down and clapped her hands three times above the water. She waited a wee while. Then lo and behold up came a big grey seal right in front of her. It never did anything, just came in right to where she sat with her coat over her behind the rock. She said, 'Will ye go and tell *Mother* that May is on the island again up to her devilment? And I want *her* to teach May a lesson she'll never forget.'

The seal never spoke, just within minutes disappeared in the water and was gone. The mother walked back to the cottage, took off the sealskin coat, hung it behind the door, sat down and picked up her knitting, smiling to herself.

Now May had been walking round the island. She had picked up a large piece of stick and was poking everything she could see, wee bleeding pappies (the sea anemones) and a jellyfish. She pulled the nippers off a crab and turned it over for the sun to get, so it's lying kicking. She enjoyed this. Then she walked further in the island to a little part that was covered in seaweed and tangles coming through a break in the rocks. Sitting there was a baby seal three or four weeks old. When she saw it she said, 'I'm going to have some fun!' So she started poking the baby seal with her stick.

It went 'hsst hsst' at her. Baby seals can't bark, they only hiss like a serpent because they're too young to have any other kind of voice. When lo and behold right at her back this voice spoke to her, 'You wicked girl, why do you do that?'

And May turned round, she looked. Standing close up behind her was a tall old woman with a long fur coat, black fur coat buttoned

right up to the neck. Her feet were in sandals and her hair was
hanging down her back in two plaits. The woman's face was as
wrinkled as a piece of old skin, but her two eyes were shining out
brown as a berry! May was surprised.

'Why do you torment the little creatures?' she said.

May said, 'It's nothing to do wi' you, old woman. Where do
you come from? You don't come from here!'

'What do *you* want coming here?' the woman said. 'This is my
place, this is *our* island!' she said.

And May said, 'I play here.'

'Well,' she said, 'you're not playing here any longer.'

'You've nothing to do with it, I'll tell my mummy about you,'
she said. 'And where do you come from anyway?'

'I know your mummy,' she said, 'and I know your sister. They
are nice persons. But you are evil.'

'What do ye want from me?'

She said, 'I'm wanting nothing *from* you; I want you!' And just
like that before May could move the old woman jumped forward and
snapped her by the wrist. It felt like a band of steel going round her
arm. She caught her, held her tight.

'Let me go,' she said, 'let me go, I'll tell my mother!'

She said, 'Don't worry about your mother. I know yer mother
perfectly well and yer sister. But you, you must come with me!'

May tried her best to get her arm out of the old woman's
grasp, but she held her in a vice grip of steel, though never hurt her.
May couldn't move. The more she pulled the worse it got. 'P-please,'
she said, 'let me go! I want to go home. Where are ye taking me to?'

The old woman said, 'I want you to come and meet my
children. How you've tortured little creatures on this island is terrible!
You ought to feel ashamed of yersel.'

She said, 'I don't feel no shame, I feel nothing. They're just
little sea people, they should be tormented.'

'Well,' she said, 'you need to be tormented! You must come
with me.' The old woman half carried, half dragged her. May was
trying to pull back but she was led further and further into the island,
over rocks and through seaweed right to the end, a place May had
never seen before. They came to a large pool that was left by the tide
and surrounded by rocks. May looked and was surprised: sitting
round the pool were four little girls. They looked identical, you
couldn't pick one from the other. The old woman said, 'Look, I want
ye to come and meet my children!'

68

'I don't want to see any children,' she said, 'I want to go home to my mother.'

She said, 'You're not going home to your mother no way – till you have learnt yer lesson.' So the old woman led May forward. In one hand she carried a walking stick. But this was not a natural stick; it was made from a large dried tangle, one of the dulse tangles people gather to make perfume. By the other hand she led May closer to the pool where these four young girls were sitting, beautiful and identical to each other, about the same age as May.

May's pulling against the old woman trying her best to escape from the grasp, 'Please, let me go back to my mummy, my mummy!'

'Evil child,' she said, 'you can't go. You've got to come here and meet my children.' She forced her to sit at the side of the large pool, three or four feet deep and two or three yards across. 'Now,' she said, 'why couldn't you, May, be like your mother and your sister? You wouldnae need to be here today – to go in this pool!'

May said, 'You're not putting me in any pool!'

'Yes,' she said, 'you're going in this pool. Because I'm going to see that you suffer the same way you made the little creatures on this island suffer. These children of mine are going to do the same thing to you that you have done to all these little creatures.'

'Oh please, please,' she said, 'don't do that to me!'

'Well,' she said, 'you've done it to them. Why shouldn't it be done to you? First we're going to put you in the pool, then you're going to become a crab and these little girls are going to pull off yer legs, pull off yer nippers. And see how you feel!'

'Oh please,' said May, 'please, please not . . . I don't want to –'

'Well,' she said, 'you did it to the crabs didn't you? Then *you're* going to become a cockle, and this one girl is going to smash ye against a stone. See how you feel then! Then you're going to be a jellyfish, and this girl here is going to poke holes in *you* with a stick. See how you feel! Then you're going to become a starfish and this one here is going to chop off yer legs with a stone – the same as you did!'

'Oh please, please, old woman,' she said, 'I couldn't stand it! Please let me go back to my mother.'

'Now children,' she said to the young ones, 'are you ready?' But they never spoke, never said a word. 'I think we'll start.'

May went down on her knees. But the old woman held her. And May begged mercy, swore she would never again touch another creature in the sea if the old woman would let her go.

So the old woman said, 'Well, seeing that your mother is a kindly soul and your sister is the nicest creature that walks this earth and hurts nobody, I'll give you one more chance! *But you must pay for your wickedness.*'

'Please,' she said, 'let me go. I'll never be wicked again, I'll not even come to the island.'

'Oh,' the old woman said, 'ye can come to the island. Join your sister gathering cockles to your heart's content, but you must learn to be good, leave the little creatures on the island alone.'

May begged from her heart and the old woman finally relented.

She turned round, 'All right, children, ye can be gone!' And just like that the four little girls disappeared over behind a rock. May never saw what happened. But these four little girls turned into seals and swam away in the water. The old woman still held her by the wrist, walked her back to the bay. 'Now,' she said, 'May, I know yer mother,' and she smiled to herself. 'And I know yer sister. I'm giving you one more chance. But ye have to pay for what ye've done in the past. You go home to your mother right now. Never let me see you doing another bad thing on this island as long as you live.' She let go her arm. And the old woman stood with her stick in the sand made of a hard black tangle.

May was glad to get free. She ran as fast as she could across the bay. But something in her mind told her to stop – she looked back in case the old woman was following her. The old woman was gone . . . there was not a soul in sight. May ran all the way with her bare feet, and when she landed in her mother's house she was exhausted. May was as white as a ghost, shaking and terrified. Her mother just sat knitting by the fireside and her sister June was sitting reading a book. May was in such a state she couldn't even talk.

The mother looked at her and just smiled, 'Well, May, where have you been?'

She said, 'I-I've b-been on the island, Mother, and I had a t-terrible experience. I had a terrible experience on the island.'

'Were ye up to yer old tricks again, May,' she said, 'hurting little creatures?'

'Yes, Mother,' she said, 'I-I was hurting little creatures, I was really. But I'll never hurt them again.'

Her mother said, 'Come down here beside me and tell me all about it.'

'But Mother,' she said, 'I'm too terrified . . . they wanted me to be a crab and they wanted me to be a jellyfish!'

But the mother never asked any questions, no way. She didn't even want to hear the story. She said, 'June, bring your sister something to eat.'

'Mother,' she said, 'I can't eat, I can't eat, Mother. I just want to be beside you, Mother. I feel terrible, I feel awful.' And then May stepped by her mother. Behind where her mother was sitting knitting was a big wardrobe and on it was a large mirror. May looked in the mirror – to her horror her beautiful hair which had been like her mother's and like her sister June's was turned snow white – as grey as grey could be, like a sheep! She started to scream, 'Mummy, Mummy, Mummy, look at me, Mummy, look at me!'

Her mother turned round to her, 'What's the matter with you, May? You look all right to me.'

'Mother, Mother!' she said. 'Look at my hair, look, my hair is grey. It's grey!'

And her mother smiled again, said, 'Come here, May, and sit on my knee.' She put May on her knee and May was shaking with the fright, terrified.

'Mummy, Mummy, my beautiful hair is gone. My hair – it's grey. I could never survive like this, Mummy. What can I do?'

'Well,' she said, 'you would neither listen to me nor listen to your sister. You're only getting paid for your evil towards the little creatures on the island.'

'But Mummy, I can't go round the world with my hair . . . I'm like an old woman!'

She said, 'May, come closer and I'll tell ye a story.' May cuddled in and sat shaking on her mother's knee. She said, 'May, I had the same experience as you a long time ago. I was wicked just like you.'

'But Mother,' she said, 'your hair is beautiful, your hair is lovely, Mother!'

'But dearie,' she said, 'my hair wasn't as nice a long time ago as it is now. My hair was grey too when I was young, because I was wicked. And as time passed by and I changed my ways, my hair began to change. So now you've learned yer lesson. Sit here on your mummy's knee and from now on forget about being wicked! And prob'ly when ye start being good and change for the best then your hair'll come in as beautiful as mine; for everybody in the village wonders why a woman like me should have such beautiful hair.'

May began to get settled by this time. 'Is that true, Mother,' she said, 'is that true? Will the old woman never come back?'

'No, my dear,' she said, 'the old woman will never bother you any more, as long as you be kind and forget all your badness, stop torturing the little creatures on the island.'

'Mummy, Mummy,' she said, 'I'll never again do another evil thing.' And sure to her word from that day on she never did an evil thing. May helped her mother in every way in the world. Her mother just needed to speak to her once. She came to her mother and asked to do good things. She walked to the village for her mother, and was kind and nice to all the people she met. But her grey hair remained.

Then one day her mother said to June, 'I think we'll have a meal of cockles today.'

And June said, 'Yes, Mother, I'll get the cockles.'

And May said, 'Mother, yes, I would like to go along and help!'

So their mother smiled, 'Well, girls,' she said, 'I'll finish off my little bit o' knitting if youse go and gather some for supper.'

So the two girls took the basket between them, a hand on each side and walked across the bay. The window of the house was facing the bay and the mother looked out. She saw the two girls walking picking up the cockles together. She smiled and said to herself, 'At last May has learned her lesson. Her hair'll not be grey for long, in another two or three months it'll be as good as ever, just like mine.' The mother stood looking out the window and smiled to herself. Then knowing there was nobody in the house to hear, she turned round and said out loud, *'Isn't it nice when ye have silkies for friends!'* And that's the end of my story.

Hooch for Skye!

When I was about four years old I heard this story. My father told me it the first time and then my Uncle Duncan, a brother of my mother's, told it to me a couple of years later. The tale is a popular one among the Highland folk, but the travellers have their own way of telling it.

Jack stayed with his mother in this wee croft away in the west corner of Skye. And he worked around the croft here and there. So on his visits to the village he used to see this old lady at the shop, when he went to the wee shop in the store. She was always in selling eggs and things, and he fell into talk wi' her one day. She asked him his name.

He said, 'Jack they call me.'

She said, 'Where do you stay?'

He said, 'I stay away down at the end of the island wi' my mother.'

She said, 'What does your mother do?'

'My mother,' he says, 'has a wee croft down there.'

'Oh aye,' she says, 'I ken your mother. I'll tell you, are ye busy?'

'No,' he said, 'my mother's wee puckle hay is cut and she's no doing very much just now.'

'Well, look,' she says, 'my old sister and me stay away down at the end o' the island, about ten miles from here. When ye go home would ye ask yer mother if she could let ye off for a couple o' days to come down and give us a wee hand wi' the hay? Because we've an awful crop o' hay this year and we canna work it wirsels, seein my old sister's gettin kind o' bad in her legs.'

'Okay,' he says, 'I'll see my mother.'

She says, 'I ken yer mother fine but it's years and years since I've seen her.'

Very well, Jack goes away home wi' his mother's bits o'

messages. Back he goes to the wee croft, into his house and his mother says, 'Well, laddie, ye're home.'

'Aye,' Jack says, 'I'm home, Mother. But Mother, a funny thing happened to me today down at the wee store where I was down at the shop. I met an old friend of yours, she's an old woman.'

'Oh,' she says, 'I ken who ye met up wi' – old Maggie. And she has an old sister Jeannie. I've never seen them for years. Jack, what was she saying to ye? Ye ken, there are a lot o' stories goes about the island about them pair.'

'Ah, Mother,' he said, 'she's a nice old woman, the nicest old woman! In fact, she wants me to come and work wi' her.'

'What!' says the mother, 'gang an work wi' her? Well, Jack, laddie, but ye can please yersel if you want to go and work with her or no. But wi' the cracks and tales that I've heard about them, they're supposed to be witches, the two o' them. And if ye're going –'

'Mother, it's for nae harm,' he says. 'The old woman only wants me to gang an' work for a couple of days wi' them at the hay. Ye ken I'm no doin much here.'

'Oh well, it's up to yersel. But,' she says, 'I'm telling you, you'd better just be careful and watch what they give ye to eat, and watch what they tell ye to do. And pay attention, because they're definitely witches!'

'Ach, Mother,' he says, 'witches! There's nae such a thing as witches nowadays.'

Anyway, the next morning his mother makes him up a bit piece and that, and he has a good bit to go, about ten mile o' a walk to the end o' the island. Away he goes, travels on and on and on; it was a lovely day, the sun was shining. He walks on, comes right down through a wee village and down to this wee croft at the side o' the shore. Up he goes an knocks at the door. The old woman comes out to him.

'Oh, it's you John,' she says. (She cried him John at first.) 'Come on in! I'm just getting my old sister up, old Jeannie, and giving her her breakfast.' She sits him down to the table and gives him a good breakfast. She says, 'Go round the shed there and ye'll get a scythe.' It was all the scythes they used in the olden days for cutting their hay. 'And there's a sharpening stone for sharpening it hangin in a leather case from the rafters. Ye'll get rakes and forks an everything else ye need in the shed. I'll give ye a wee shout at dinner-time.'

'All right,' says Jack.

Jack got used to this farm working, kent all about it. It was

74

just a wee two or three acres of hay. They kept yin cow and a puckle hens these two old sisters; they sold eggs and things. He worked away all day, cut all this hay for them. He nearly finished it.

The old sister came out and gave him a shout, 'Come on in, Jack! It's about dinner-time.'

In he comes, sits down. He looks. He's never seen the other old sister before, but she's sitting at the table. He looks at her.

'Aye,' Maggie says, 'you've never met my sister, Jack. That's my sister Jeannie there. She's kind o' deaf, she'll no hear ye. She's two-three years older than me. Her legs are kind o' bad.'

'Well,' he says, 'I didna get your hay finished. I dinna ken if it's going to come on rain or no. And there's a lot –'

'Dinna worry, laddie! Dinna go home tonight!' Maggie says. 'There's plenty of room for you – ye can stay here. I'll make you a nice bed at the kitchen fire. Your mother'll ken where ye are. She'll no worry about ye.'

'All right,' says Jack. But anyway, Jack goes away out again, works another half day.

But he thought to himself, 'There's something funny about that old sister o' hers. She says she's older than her, but she looks younger than her. And the way I saw her moving her feet in alow the table, there's no much wrong wi' her legs! And she disna use a staff because there's no a staff lying against the table. There's something kind o' droll – I canna figure it out. But anyway I'll mind what my mother tellt me,' so he's thinking.

But he works on again till five o'clock. The old woman gives him a shout, takes him in, gives him his supper. Now it be coming on late in the year, the hay was late, it was about September month. The nights were coming in close. The two old women made a bed to Jack at the front o' the fire, put a big fire o' peats on. And they went away up the stairs to their bed. Jack fell asleep.

He's lying and the fire's burning down low, ken, when the peats burn down low it's just a red *grìosach*, a red fire. And he hears the feet coming down, two old sisters coming walking down the stairs. They come right to the fire. And old Jeannie, the one who was supposed to be crippled says, 'He's sleeping, he'll no hear you, he's sleeping.'

Jack was lying, and he lifted the blanket a wee bit, he keeked out. This is the two old sisters, and the other ane is walking as good as you and me! They go over to the side o' the grate. And there's an oven at the side of the grate. They open the door of the oven, and they take out a red cowl. (That's a kind o' woolly bonnet or 'toorie' with a long tassel on it.) One pulls one right down over her hair, the other one takes another one out and she pulls it over *her* hair. And they say, 'Hooch for London!' They're gone – both of them were gone!

Jack got up, wandered around the house, lighted a lamp, searched the house upside down outside in, but na! Round to the byre, the cow was standing eating at the back of the byre. Right round the hayfield, he searched round the place. The two old sisters were gone, there was not a bit to be seen o' them! So he searched round and round every shed, every nook, into the hen house, round the fields, down to the well – not a soul to be seen. The two old sisters had completely vanished, he couldn't find them anywhere.

He goes back into the house, kindles up the fire and makes himself a cup of tea. 'Man,' he says to himself, 'I doubt my mother was right. Where could those two old women go to this time o' night?' He looks at the clock. It was dead on twelve o'clock when they left, and now it was near one in the morning. Still no signs o' them. 'Ach,' he says, 'it'll no matter. I canna explain it. Maybe my mother'll tell me. But anyway I'm going to see it through, I'm going to see what happens here, I'm no going home till I see what happens.'

But he put some more peats on the fire, went back to his bed and happed himself up. But he must have fallen asleep. He was sleeping for about a couple o' hours when he heard the door opening. In came the first sister, and in came the second sister walking as good as me and you! Each had a bag in their hand, a leather bag. They placed them down on the table. And it was 'clink'. With the way they clinked it was money that was in the bags.

So one says to the other, 'Jeannie, one for you, one for me. Put them back in the same place where we put the rest!'

'Right!' Away goes old Jeannie up the stairs with the two bags and puts them away.

Jack's lying, he never says a word. The other old sister comes over and she stands aside the fire, she listen to see if she could hear him. She says to herself, 'He's sleeping, he's never wakened, he disna ken the difference.' She went away up the stairs, closed the door and all was silent.

But anyway, Jack fell asleep and he must have slept on. The first thing that wakened him was the old wife giving him a shout in the morning. She said, 'Jack, it's time to get up, seven o'clock, rise and get your breakfast!'

'Okay,' he said, 'I'll get up.' Jack got up, put on his clothes, had a wash. The old wife came round, gave him a good breakfast, porridge an milk an eggs.

She said, 'How are you this morning, Jack? Did ye sleep well last night? Anything disturb ye during the night?'

'Not a thing disturbed me during the night,' he said, 'I slept like a lamb the whole night through.'

'That's good,' she says, 'you must have been working hard.'

But anyway, Jack goes out, sharpens his scythe. Out to the field, starts again, cuts away an cuts away, finishes the hay. All the hay is lying out.

Old Maggie comes out, gives him a shout again. 'Come on in, Jack, it's about dinner-time!'

He comes, gets his dinner, sits an cracks to them for a long long while. They ask him about his mother and all these things, about his croft, one thing and another until the dinner hour is up. 'Ah well,' he says, 'I'll have to go away back out an get on with the work.'

So he went out and he started turning the hay. It was a lovely sunny day. He worked away till night-time again. He came in, had his supper. To make a long story short it came to bedtime again. The two old sisters bade him good-night. Jack made his bed by the fire and he lay down. He looked at the clock, an old wag-at-the-wall clock was what they had on the wall. Half past eleven . . . Jack's sound in bed.

But just on the chap o' twelve o'clock he hears the feet coming down the stairs again. Down they come. One says to the other, 'Is he sleeping?'

She says, 'He's sound. He must have worked hard today, but we'll make it worth his while. We'll give him a good pay.'

He's lying, Jack's lying, he hears every word. Up they go again to the grate, open the door of the oven. Out comes the two cowls, on to their heads, 'Hooch for London!' They're off, off they go!

Same thing happened again. Jack got up, searched the house upside down, went up the stairs. The door to their bedroom was locked. 'Now,' he said, 'I cannae break the door down – they'll ken I was up the stairs.' He searched the house upside and down and he found this key. He tried it and the door opened. He went into their bedroom, and round the whole room. And in alow the bed he pulled out this big box, a leatherbound trunk. It was packed with wee bags, and every single bag was full o' sovereigns, gold sovereigns! 'Hmm,' he said, 'there's as much money there as would do everybody in the Isle of Skye!' And he shoved it back in below their bed, shut the door, locked it, put the key back where he had found it. He went away back down, back to his bed, fell sound asleep. He never heard them coming back.

The next morning they came down and wakened him again. She said, 'Had you a good sleep last night, Jack?'

'Oh, I slept,' he said, 'I was tired, dead tired. I'll finish the hay today, and –'

'Ah, but you'll have to put it up in ricks for us,' she says, 'because it will be wet lying like that, and ye ken you'll have to put it in stacks for us and do a bit o' repairs before you go away home, fencing an that. I can employ you for a week, ye can stay a week. Your mother kens where you are so she'll no worry about you.'

He's thinking to himself now, 'Where they go tonight, I'm going with them!'

'Oh but,' she says, 'I forgot to tell you, Jack, there's a lot o' clothes here about your size that belonged to my brother. He was just about your age when he was killed, and there's a lot o' stuff here that's nae use to me and my old sister. We'll look it out for ye and you'll take it home wi' ye, it'll do for working wi'. My brother was killed.'

He says, 'What happened to your brother?'

'Oh,' she says, 'he was killed down in London. Anyway, we'll no speak about that.'

So Jack works all day, comes in, has his dinner. Works on in the afternoon again, has his supper. And he comes back in, goes to his bed.

Twelve o'clock he hears the feet coming down the stairs. He says, 'Where they're going tonight I'm going with them!'

One old sister says to the other, 'I think he's sleeping, he's no moving.' Over to the side of the fire they go, open the door beside the wee grate, pull out the cowls – on their heads – 'Hooch for London!'

Jack gets up out o' the bed, runs to the fire, he opens the oven and there's one red toorie left. He pulls it on his head, 'Hooch for London!' he says. 'Hooch for London!'

He travelled through the air at about a hundred miles an hour wi' this cowl on his head and the two sisters in front o' him. They circled round London, and down – right through this window! And with the welt he got coming down, he didna ken any words to stop himself for landing, he was knocked out completely. See, they knew words for to cushion their blow, how to land, but he didnae. He landed after them. When he wakened up, you know where he was lying? He was lying inside a cellar in the Royal Mint, and he was surrounded by thousands o' bags of gold sovereigns! And his toorie was gone. So were the two old sisters. They were gone. But this is where they had been going, robbing the mint every night. Two witches!

But Jack searched all around . . . the mint's locked, there's no way o' him getting out – impossible! So in the morning when the guards came down they got him sitting inside the mint. Now this was what had happened to their brother before, to the sisters' old brother. Oh, Jack's in a terrible state now – he disna ken what to do with himself!

So the guards they ask him how he got in. But he couldn't explain, he says he disna ken how he got in. So in those days for stealing out o' the mint, the penalty was death, sentenced to death. You were hanged in an open court out in the front o' the public square. Jack is arrested, taken out of the cellar o' the mint, taken up to the court, tried and sentenced to be hanged for robbing the Royal Mint. And so many dozens o' bags of gold that had gone a-missing – he got the blame o' the lot.

But anyway, he lay in the jail for three days, till the day he was to be hanged. He was taken out, taken up the steps, the thirteen steps to the scaffold and put on the scaffold. The hangman came, put the rope round his neck. And the minister came up to say two or three words to him before they hanged him.

The minister says to Jack, 'John, you were sentenced to death for robbing the Royal Mint. Have you anything to say before ye get hanged?' When up the steps to the scaffold runs this old lady!

She says to the hangman, 'Yes, I've got something to say!' And she placed the cowl on Jack's head. 'Hooch for Skye!' she said. The two of them were off!

And when Jack wakened up he was lying at the side of the fire back in the two old sisters' croft. As he wakens up this old sister's shouting to him, 'Jack, get up! It's time to get on wi' your work!'

So Jack worked all week for the two old sisters, forgot all about it. He said, 'I must have been dreaming – that never really happened to me – I must have been dreaming. Or was my mother right . . . did I dream or did it really happen? But anyway I must ask them!' At the end of the week he said to the two old sisters, 'Was I ever out o' here?'

'No,' she says, 'Jack, ye werena out o' here. You worked well. You've been the best worker ever we had here, you did everything!'

'But,' he says, 'was I no away from here, this place, during the night or anything? Did anything funny happen?'

'Na! You slept like a lamb o' God,' she says. 'You never were away from this place. Every morning we came down at breakfast time you were aye lying in your bed, and you were lying in your bed when we went to our bed at night. You've never been out of this place since you came – for a full week.'

'Ah well, that's funny . . . ach,' he says, 'it must hae been a dream I had. I dreamed that I landed in . . .' he tellt her the whole story, he landed in the mint and he was to be hanged till death. 'And you,' he says, 'came.'

'Ach, Jack,' she says, 'you've been dreaming! The same thing happened to my poor brother, he had a dream like that too. But that's the last we ever saw o' him.'

So the old sister went away to get something for Jack, something for his breakfast. And he opened the oven and he keeked in, and inside the oven were three red toories, inside the oven. He said, 'I wasna dreaming.' And he shut the door. She came back in.

'Well,' he says to the old sister, 'that's all your jobs finished now. I think it's about time that I went home to see how my old mother's getting on.'

'Ah, but Jack,' she says, 'my sister has made up that bundle o' clothes for you that belonged to my brother. I think they'll do ye, just the very thing, you're about his build. Wait, I'll go an get ye your pay!'

So they gave him this big bundle of clothes to take back with him for his work. The two sisters went up the stairs and the one came down. She's carrying these two wee leather bags in her hand. 'There,' she said, 'Jack, there's your pay. And that's as much that'll keep you and your old mother for the rest o' your days.'

And Jack went away home to his mother and stayed happy for ever after. And that's the last o' the wee story!